Land's End to John o' Groats

On a beer mat

ISBN: 978-1-326-44859-2

Cover design by Dave Lewis
Photographs by Dave Lewis, Derek Goode, Sue Gurman and a
number of very kind passers by

Also available as an e-book

For more information contact the author here:
www.david-lewis.co.uk

Published in the UK by www.publishandprint.co.uk

Special thanks to Sue for letting me go, and Derek for coming
with me

Dave Lewis

Land's End to John o' Groats

On a beer mat

Publish & Print
www.publishandprint.co.uk

For Dad

Bicycle bicycle bicycle
I want to ride my bicycle bicycle bicycle
I want to ride my bicycle
I want to ride my bike
I want to ride my bicycle
I want to ride my

Bicycle races are coming your way
So forget all your duties oh yeah!
Fat bottomed girls they'll be riding today
So look out for those beauties oh yeah

On your marks get set go

- Freddie Mercury

Land's End to John o' Groats

Background

It was in a curryhouse in Taffs Well, sometime in May 2005, when my girlfriend announced to me, in the presence of two of our best friends, that we should get married. I nearly choked on my Chicken Tikka Dupiaza! I wish she'd waited until I'd finished my meal at least.

I quickly sank the dregs of my Kingfisher lager, gulped some much-needed oxygen into my lungs, went ashen white and mumbled an incoherent reply.

'Hang on Sue! Let's not rush into anything, is it?'

Alun and Sian were laughing so much they nearly fell off their chairs!

What could I say? I'd had a good innings as they say. We'd been going out forever. Well, fifteen years or so anyway. Some people get less for murder I'd heard. But there were other reasons of course...

In 2002 I'd become a dad and our precious miracle baby; who'd somehow ignored the sterilisation and lack of a full compliment of fallopian tubes in my wife-to-be, needed a married mam and dad. At least that's what my mam and dad thought, worried that our happy hippy existence wasn't the best way to bring up a child in 21st Century Wales these days.

There was another reason too.

1

My dad had been diagnosed with terminal lung cancer and it was only a matter of time. So, with a heavy heart and a thousand emotions swirling around inside my mostly empty head what could I do?

'Brilliant idea love!'

'You don't look well Dave,' said Alun, still smirking like Shrek.

The wedding was to be a small affair. Registry office, two witnesses; Alun and Sian, two bridesmaids; our respective daughters, plus my mam and dad. We told no-one. Sue planned and arranged it all. I bought an orange shirt from a trendy clothes shop I'd never be seen in again and the kids; Eve and Eleri, got excited about dressing up in their frilly little numbers. God they start early eh!

Such was my state of shock in the weeks leading up to this monumentus occasion that I needed constant liquid sustenance. I also wouldn't have survived the ordeal without continuous reassurance from our friends, funny stories from Mark, a dose of glandular fever, some double pneumonia that nearly killed me and five days in hospital, you know, the usual things.

And so it was, over a few pints, then a few pints more, with my secret still in tact, during one such male bonding session that me and Derek started talking about cycling.

Enter the beer mat...

Now I don't know what Ranulph Fiennes does when he begins to plan an epic adventure but I'm sure he could have avoided frostbite and sawing his own fingers off if only he'd scribbled down a few ideas on a beer mat before setting sail for the land of penguins and yellow popsicles. For example, he could have written, in a leaky biro from behind the bar of the Llanover Arms, Pontypridd - 'Don't get frostbite' - and that would have surely saved himself a lot of trouble in the digit department.

As for me and Derek, well, we should have written - 'Don't buy a Dawes bike' or 'Do some training first' or 'Make sure you book some B&Bs'. Actually, looking back, I think we needed a few beer mats but hindsight is a wonderful thing.

So, having got married and missed the impromptu party that started in our house after someone spotted us all dressed up ('What? Dave in a shirt?' someone said) taking photographs over Pontypridd Common, me and my new wife contemplated life apart for two weeks on our brief, one-night honeymoon in an old country house somewhere between Brecon and Crickhowell, kindly paid for by Alun and Sian.

Initial Planning... Lol

'Derek, you're drunk!' I slurred.

'Not as drunk as you are Dave,' came the reply about three minutes later.

'Yeh, but I haven't been on a bike for ages. Years in fact. In fact I think it was twenty years ago. It may have been longer than that in fact.'

'Stop stating facts,' said Derek.

'Yeh, well, anyway, I have bad knees, so it wouldn't work,' I continued.

'You'll be fine Dave. I used to go fishing to the reservoir with my knees and I always got lost on the way home,' added Derek reassuringly.

'OK, you've convinced me mate. So we're going then!'

'When?'

'Now, in a minute... oh shit no we can't, I haven't got a bike yet.'

'OK, we better get a curry then first.'

'Yep, they don't strike me as cyclists though, too much beards. Think about it. You'd never win the Tour de France with a beard.'

'Unless you were French, then you might.'

'Or Spanish.'

'Papadums?'

'No, Sue will drive, or Gosia, yeh, sorted.'

'Do Italians still have beards?'

We stood to leave.

'Don't forget that beer mat. We don't want to go without that.'

'Hic.'

In Depth Planning... Kind Of

After frantically scribbling last minute preparations onto the back of our now very sodden and worn out beer mat we racked the bikes and headed for Cornwall.

The Challenge - to test our prostates over a gruelling two-week course dressed only in Lycra and a spare pair of socks, just in case we needed to impress any ladies en-route.

I did the tour t-shirts (the really tough job) and Derek was left with the easy task of sorting through maps, weather reports, hill profiles, alternative routes, possible accommodation stops, bike shops, corner shops, shops not on corners, the daily Ceefax wind directions and loads of other non-essential stuff.

The plan was, albeit a bit sketchy, for us to start at Land's End, Cornwall, get on our bikes, cycle for a bit, then hopefully, if all things went well, finish up at John o' Groats, Caithness a bit later.

We hoped to cover approximately 950 miles (although at the time this didn't include Derek's attraction to Gloucester) and also thought it would be a great idea to raise some money for Ty-Hafan - the children's hospice in Wales.

The Route - supplementary beer mats would show that we did indeed decide on a route before leaving, which we got from the 'Bike Britain' book by Paul Salter, although Derek found quite a few detours in order to add some big hills (the utter bastard!) and take in some different scenery.

As for the state-of-the-art equipment we would need to complete this epic challenge, well, I bought a Dawes Discovery 701 for £600 by Googling a few bike reviews. Again, thinking back it would probably have been a better idea to have actually sat on a bike before I bought one but I just love the Internet! Anyway, they were out of stock but undeterred I said I'd wait. Eventually it turned up, flat-packed like an Ikea wardrobe... oh dear. Great bike though as long as you get the wheels with lots of spokes, not the sporty ones I had (more on that later). My experienced cycling companion, Derek, went for the trusty (or should that be rusty?) ten year old, second-hand Raleigh with the only adaptations being a 36-tooth gear set for the hills kindly donated by Mr Eddie Woodman of Maesycoed and a rear pannier rack from his father.

'Bloody professional!' I shouted.

Digs - this was our biggest expense as 'rip-off' Britain is so extortionate for accommodation. We decided the best way of coping with this was to not bother. That way we could appeal to the good nature of our fellow Britons who we decided would never leave this dynamic duo, cycling for a worthy children's charity, stranded for the night and would move heaven and earth to find room at the inn for us... Mmm? Who were we kidding?

We did get a £10 sponsorship from the Kellsboro Hotel in Newquay which was very nice though, so thank you to them!

We also booked the first night and our last two nights, which kinda gave us a target to aim for.

6

Training - as every serious athlete knows, training is paramount. So coupled with a special scientific nutritional diet of real ale and curry we devised a strenuous regime, guaranteed to push us to our very limits. Well, Derek did anyway. I just kinda turned up at sixteen and a half stone and moaned about my old rugby injuries.

We did manage a forty-four mile ride, around Brecon two weeks before we set off, when my new bike finally arrived from the Internet, and boy was my bum sore! I kept wondering how Edward II felt (OK, maybe not). Other than that though I did nothing.

'Are you sure you're up for this Dave?' asked Derek.

'Del, don't worry, I'll do my training on the way,' I replied, not knowing just how numb a bottom could get at this particular moment in history.

Transport - lifts needed organising of course. We needed someone to drop us off in Land's End with the bikes and some real mugs to drive all the way to John o' Groats to fetch us back, if we ever made it that far.

Luckily for me I had just acquired a wife and this was a really handy thing to have whenever you had to get a lift anywhere. So it was decided that Sue would drop us off at Cornwall while Alun and Mark would pick us up in Scotland with a hire car kindly donated by Europcar, thanks to some dodgy civil service deal we won't go into here. The downside of this was that it meant we'd be carrying all our kit with us, the whole way, which was bound to slow us down. Well it would if we took a change of clothes. Right, another decision made then.

Charity - as stated earlier we thought if we're going to put ourselves through hell then why not do it for a good cause. We argued about this for a bit (I wanted to save elephants and rhinos) but eventually decided it would have to be a local Welsh charity.

We somehow managed to 'organise' a disco and a few beers at a local pub, Clwb Y Bont, Pontypridd, who kindly donated the use of the backroom to us for free, and we even managed to raise nearly £750 thanks to the generosity of our friends, family and half the local Polish population who we told there might be vodka in the raffle prizes.

Kit List

X1 Bike (Dawes Discovery 701) - great bike, shame about the racing wheels

X1 Helmet - Halfords own, neither of us being that fashion conscious

X1 Spare inner tube - Halfords again, all rubbers look the same once inside

X1 Puncture repair kit (with tyre levers) - they never work do they!

X1 Pannier rack with two small panniers - not waterproof

X2 Water bottles - to put our Lucozade in

X1 Bike computer - Halfords own, so we know exactly how much more punishment is to come

X1 Cycling top - borrowed from a friend

X2 Elasticated cycling shorts - Aldi's finest, why pay more?

X2 Pairs walking socks - Bridgedale, 'cos I'm worth it

X1 Karrimor walking shoes - before they went bust, got took over by some crappy Sports chain and became crap

X1 Waterproof (ish) coat - from Up & Under, Cardiff, tidy mun

X1 Cycling gloves - Aldi again

X3 Pants - one on, one spare, one for Sunday best

X2 T-shirts - for pub in night (took two just in case someone caught us wearing the same outfit twice, 'cos I'd simply die)

X1 Sandals / flip-flops - to air the feet after all day cycling in the walking shoes

X1 Small compact camera - 'cos digital was too expensive back in 2005

X2 35mm film, Fuji 200 ISO - nicer blues and quite sharp I always found

X1 Mobile - 'cos I had to start somewhere with technology

X1 'Curry card' (i.e. Lloyds bank Visa / cashpoint card) - for B&Bs and buying spare wheels

X1 Bike Britain paperback - so we knew which way was north

X1 Diary / pen - so I could write about all the things that went wrong

X2 Plastic bags - to put pants and t-shirts in when we had really heavy rain

X1 Shower gel (small) - to keep the weight down

X1 Toothpaste (small) / brush - ditto

X1 Sun cream F30 (small) - in Britain, lol, ditto

X1 Toilet roll - in case I got caught short on the moors, which I did, but I'd lost the toilet roll so had to use my pants and throw them away but I figured cotton was bio-degradable so it was alright

Penzance, Cornwall
Friday 1st July 2005
Pontypridd to Penzance (by car)

We began our expedition in the year of our lord 2005, in the summer month of July, about dinnertime, after literally minutes of serious training and rigorous preparation. The only training ride we'd managed was the forty-four mile trip from Brecon to Pontypridd (down the Taff Trail) over two weeks ago but whilst we hadn't really taken that very seriously, last night we did. Thursdays are not usually that mental in the south Wales valleys but we'd thoroughly enjoyed our quiet six pint binge with curry nightcap in order to fully relax us for the safari ahead.

OK, it probably wasn't the best preparation for our epic journey but on the other hand it does go to prove that any idiot can do this ride! And I guess that is the whole point of this account.

Up at nine o'clock, I took the dog for a walk, came back and packed my panniers. Then I worried that I was taking too much. After all, it was only going to be two weeks if all went well...

I cycled to Derek's house and was knackered by the time I got there. He does live about four miles away from me though so this was to be expected. Oh dear.

It was tipping down with rain as we packed the car and we finally managed to leave Pontypridd by half past one. I calculated it would be a swift three-hour drive to Penzance, a town and port in Cornwall, a few miles inland from our true destination - Land's

End. It took us five hours and when we finally got to our hostel we were shattered.

'Smiling Because We Hadn't Sat On A Saddle Yet'

Outside the digs in Penzance

Modern humans recolonized Cornwall after the last Ice Age. Cornwall in the Late Bronze Age was part of a large maritime trading network with Ireland, England, France, Spain and Portugal. Like most of Britain south of the Firth of Forth, Cornwall was Celtic and culturally very close to Wales and Brittany. The language spoken at the time eventually developed into Cornish.

Even today Cornwall is recognised by several organisations, including the Cornish nationalist party Mebyon Kernow, the Celtic League and the International Celtic Congress, as one of the six Celtic nations, alongside Brittany, Ireland, the Isle of Man, Scotland and Wales.

Cornwall also has its own flag, a white cross on a black background. The Saint Piran's Flag is regarded by many as the national flag of Cornwall, and an emblem of the Cornish people; and by others as the county flag.

Penzance is well known for being the most westerly town in Cornwall and is approximately 300 miles west-southwest of London. Situated in the shelter of Mount's Bay, the town faces southeast onto the English Channel. Penzance is known as 'holy headland' in the Cornish language, a reference to the location of a chapel nowadays called St Anthony's that is said to have stood over a thousand years ago on the headland to the west of what became Penzance Harbour. However like many Celtic traditions there are few documents left to offer support to this story and so it might just be complete bollocks. It's the same in Wales. We all know the Ark of the Covenant is buried somewhere in Ynysybwl but no-one else seems to believe us when we mention it. Well, all I can say is 'I told you so' when it finally gets discovered. Anyway if the rest of the world doesn't care, neither do we.

But I digress. Back in 2005 the July weather was the usual mix of rain and heavy rain with some light drizzle thrown in for good measure as we found the backpackers at 6:30pm and were checked in by Stuart, a young, *old Rhodie* who informed us that he'd never died and then sang a song about when we was Rhodesia everything worked and... Anyway, myself, Sue and little Eve (three years old) were

13

given a dorm for £41 (without breakfast) to which I screamed 'What? For a hostel! I hate rip-off Britain - it's shit!'

Once I'd unpacked (i.e. thrown my panniers on the floor) we met up with Derek and wandered along the seafront, the damp drizzle turning to slightly wetter rain. We had an overpriced meal and then an overpriced pint of St Austells at the Dolphin Tavern. The food was good in fairness although Derek didn't finish his beer as he had a really bad stomach, probably due to last night's curry (I made a mental note not to slipstream him on the morrow). He went on the whisky instead. So with toddler Eve too tired for us to sink many more beers it was early to bed by ten o'clock. We all tucked ourselves in (not all in the same bed I might add) as Derek continued to moan about his dodgy belly, the wimp!

Day One
Saturday 2nd July 2005
Land's End to Newquay (by bike from now on...)

Didn't sleep much. Woke at five o'clock in huge anticipation to heavy drizzle. You know, that really wet sort of rain that soaks through to your bones and makes you feel miserable for days. We had nowhere to lock our bikes up last night so left them outside. We were amazed that they were still there but even that didn't put us off.

'Not Happy That The Famous Signpost Man
Was Still Asleep'

Outside the Land's End Hotel

Derek drove us all to Land's End in his car. There we found a grey, miserable, horrible, tacky

15

touristy place with no famous signpost in sight. Great start!

We were told by a local man with his dog that the guy who owns it doesn't get up until ten o'clock - lazy bugger. He also informed us that we'd have to pay to take a photograph of the sign with our hometown / charity event info. or whatever on the signpost. I couldn't believe this as the rain began to settle in for the day.

So instead of a scrum of paparazzi we took a quick photo of us with our bikes and waterproofs outside the Land's End Hotel and wondered if we should do a Lou Reed and wait for the man. Derek popped inside the hotel to get our official forms stamped by the nice lady on the reception desk.

'Bollocks to this f***** bollocks,' I eloquently exclaimed.

'Shall we depart?' offered Derek.

'Aye, I'm not kissing this tarmac though, it's all sticky, let's go buttie. I can't believe they want to fleece you for a photo when you're doing a charity ride for a children's hospital, bloody Thatcher's Britain eh!'

'Blair's Britain mate,' corrected Derek.

I waited a few more minutes for my riding partner to faff about with mechanical bike stuff, whatever that was, accepted we'd have no inspiring photo to set us on our journey - only rain and wind - and off we set!

So, this was it. We were eventually on the road at 9:00am. 'I hate rip-off Britain - it's shit!' someone said. A theme that was to echo across vale and dale for two weeks...

16

We cycled about a mile, the rain still wet and I shouted to Derek.

'Hey Derek, guess what?'

'What's up?' he replied.

'Well, according to my bike computer we only have 999 miles to go!'

'The second word's off Dave!' as he cycled on.

Now, this is probably the time when I should mention our philosophy with regards route planning. Many cyclists decide to do the End to End ride because they are good cyclists, very fit and want to challenge themselves to see how fast they can do it. Personally, I think that's fine, but why risk life and limb on the great British roads? Why not go to the gym and jump on a bike and cycle 900 miles or so? Same result - a time to impress your two friends with.

Now whilst Derek is a very good cyclist, he's since done the Carten (Cardiff to Tenby) loads of times, the Wales Velothon, the Dragon, Tour de France etc. I'm certainly not! The whole point of us doing the End to End was to see as much of our great country by bike. Yes it was a challenge, yes it was bloody hard, yes we kept stats but more than that it was a chance to do something a bit special.

So, the route we decided upon was: mostly B roads, 'that pub looks nice', 'that seems like an interesting town', 'some bloke said to go here', in other words anything a bit different...

We started with some gentle ups and downs, then found some more serious ups and downs - great! We descended to St Just, which is a lovely, little, secret cove of a place. Then we made the popular bay of St Ives, which is nice, although a bit touristy, probably due to all the artists that live here now. It wasn't always like this though as the town was founded by an Irish Saint back in the 5th Century.

Then we passed through a few other saintly places like Hayle and the beautiful Portreath (meaning 'sandy cove'). Digital cameras were in their early days in 2005 and I relied on a cheap 35mm compact. Problem was, as a photographer, I kept stopping to take photos, which slowed our pace quite a bit and caused Derek's ever-present grin to vanish on quite a few occasions.

'One Of Many Ups Amongst The Downs'

St Ives, Cornwall

We watched the real surfers at Portreath during yet another Mars bar and Lucozade break.

Then we pushed on to the village of St Agnes, which is at least 12,000 years old, and stopped off at a Tesco to use some more of our huge supply of free Lucozade vouchers. I don't think the supermarket is that old though. This was where our troubles really started, because as every top athlete knows dehydration is a serious problem. But after several *buy-one-get-one-free's* we were in mortal danger of over-hydrating and we resolved to push on to Newquay and do some serious isotonic restoration via a few real ales.

Eventually we got to the pretty seaside town that shares it's name with a much nicer, much prettier seaside town in West Wales but not before one of my spokes started pinging - crappy Dawes bike that I had - buy Japanese I say! Stopped off in our first of many bike shops throughout the UK (start counting them now) and got some friendly advice from two very nice guys.

We walked through town and bumped into Sue and Eve who'd been there all day shopping, eating ice cream and looking for bronzed, hunky surfers, although Sue's reply when I pointed this out was 'Oh, I hadn't really noticed, love.'

Newquay town dates back to the Bronze Age although it was much later that an Iron Age hill fort was built near here. The medieval period saw the fishing harbour grow up thanks to the great natural setting.

These days Newquay town centre is awash with stag and hen do's and you'll struggle to see a real surfer anywhere though.

Although house prices at the pretty seaside resorts are high, Cornwall is one of the poorest parts of the United Kingdom in terms of average household incomes. It's very much like west Wales in that respect. Retired people and second-home owners drive the prices up and the locals have nowhere to live. In the wintertime many little villages are as dead as British manufacturing.

We eventually made the Kellsboro Hotel where we had a dip in the pool! Luxury!
Good first day's cycling – fifty-seven miles and fourteen hills, already the furthest I'd ever been on a bike in my life in one day! The training had begun!

Got £5 sponsorship from Paul - the nice man with the bouncy castle (Black Widow Services) - and proceeded to restore fluid levels with a Guinness in the pub next door to the hotel. After a huge cod and a pile of wedges I was exhausted and we only managed one more beer.
Dreading the days ahead we turned in early and watched Pink Floyd on telly. It was Live8, a pointless event where multi-millionaire pop stars who've never done a day's work in their lives, and understand even less about how Africa actually works, beg the UK's poor people for money to give to corrupt African dictatorships and genocidal maniacs so they can abuse their people even more than normal rather than invest in education and family planning. In fact Live Aid (which raised over $100 million) caused more deaths than it prevented but

why let the truth influence a scruffy Irishman's knighthood?

So, knowing I was knackered and extremely apprehensive at the prospect of a second day in the saddle Sue kept me awake half the night singing along to Robbie bloody Williams. And if I ever meet Robbie bloody Williams...

Cycling Stats

Start: 9:00am
Distance: 57.43 miles
Total Distance: 57.43 miles
Average Speed: 11.3 mph
Fastest Speed: 38.4 mph
Cycling Time: 5 hrs 5 mins
Finish: 4:30pm
Beers: 2

Day Two
Sunday 3rd July 2005
Newquay to Okehampton

Woke up to the sound of Eve screaming for her milkie and bottle (a kind of constant these last three years). Her cries reminiscent of Piggy's conch in William Golding's Lord of the Flies, which is interesting as he was born in Newquay. Better than Robbie bloody Williams anyway.

Up at seven o'clock and after £10 sponsorship from the owners of the hotel and a scrummy breakfast we were ready for the off with just a hint of sunshine.

Our wet clothes were almost dry, Eve was naughty, Derek fixed my spokes, Eve was naughty, said goodbyes to Sue, Eve was naughty... You're getting the picture I hope.

Plenty of steep, long uphills until we eventually got a bit of speed up going down the A39 and across the River Camel into Wadebridge, former home of the pretty sick comedian Jethro (Geoffrey Rowe). We made a Lucozade stop in the Co-op.

Tore up our first map near Camelford but didn't see any knights sat at our small, round table in the beer garden. Camelford has been linked to the legendary Camelot, although like much Arthurian history there is much speculation, debate and argument. Don't know why really, as we Welsh all know the real King Arthur was from just outside

Abercwmboi, not far from where the Stereophonics come from.

Some historians believe there were actually two or even three different 'King Arthur's'. One story has him single-handedly killing 960 men in the Battle of Badon in the 5th Century. No one seems to know where this was exactly but if it was anywhere near Merthyr or Pontypridd on a Saturday night there might well be some truth in the legend. Guess we'll never know for sure.

We cycled up a big hill out of Camelot when disaster struck! Well, I got a puncture anyway. Derek, who from now on shall be known as 'bicycle repair man' got us back on the road after the second attempt and we made it across the Tamar River to Devon - our first county photo.

'Tearing Up Our First Map To Lighten The Load'

Heading to Camelot

The name Devon derives from the name of the Britons who inhabited the southwestern peninsula of Britain at the time of the Roman conquest of Britain known as the Dumnonii, thought to mean 'deep valley dwellers' in Celtic.

Although most people just think of clotted cream and scones, Devon is most famous for its mariners. Sir Francis Drake, Sir Humphrey Gilbert, Sir Richard Grenville, Sir Walter Raleigh, Sir Francis Chichester and the notorious pirate Henry Every all hail from this fertile land.

More big climbs and some nice views of Dartmoor followed. Then we got sucked down a black hole into Okehampton, a lovely town though, founded by the Saxons in 980 AD. Stayed at my favourite place on the whole trip - an old boys school. Upcott House is set in it's own gardens and is just lovely. All in all a great day in which we covered sixty-three miles and another fourteen hills - another world record and personal best for me.

We arrived late, had a hot bath and went out. Sue rang about her day, which was just as eventful as ours, apart from the knights of the round table bit. She drove Derek's car home and decided to refuel. Eve was naughty. She stopped at a petrol station and discovered she didn't have the key to the petrol cap! Eve was naughty and wanted more milkie and bottle. Sue was not far outside Newquay when this happened and in severe need of hydrocarbons. Eve was still being naughty. Eventually a kind man informed her that the ignition key also opened the petrol cap. Panic over. Women eh!

Back in Okehampton we went to the Feather of Plumes pub for a huge slap up meal consisting of sausages (three), eggs (two), loads of baked beans and piles of chips all washed down by two pints of Guinness because like I said earlier us professional athletes need to keep our bodies in tip-top condition. After all, as pregnant women will tell you, Guinness has iron in it. Maybe only 0.3 milligrams per pint but it's a start.

Then we wandered over to the Plymouth Inn, which is just like our local, the Llanover Arms in Pontypridd, where we had more Guinness bought for us by a friendly Scottish builder from Devon who'd actually worked in Pontypridd and Beddau! In fact he knew more about Beddau than we did.

Then the night took on a sinister twist as two 'vampire' Alsatian dogs started sucking the blood from a cut on Derek's leg. I love dogs but don't think Derek is so keen which was just as well seeing as I spent the next hour trying to distract him from looking down at his oozing leg.

We talked to the owners for a bit but didn't get any sponsorship which was a bit annoying, although one of the dogs did pee all over me, which was very nice. We left slightly the worse for wear after our exertions of the day and I hoped Derek didn't turn into a bat on Dartmoor as we strolled home. I've read 'Fear and Loathing in Las Vegas' and know it doesn't end well!

Cycling Stats

Start: 9:15am
Distance: 63.61 miles
Total Distance: 121.04 miles
Average Speed: 11.3 mph
Fastest Speed: 38.6 mph
Cycling Time: 5 hrs 35 mins
Finish: 7:05pm
Beers: 4

Day Three
Monday 4th July 2005
Okehampton to Glastonbury

Woke at five o'clock in the morning again and thought that I really should shut the curtains since it was summertime. Up at seven o'clock, quick breakie and left the lovely little B&B. Last night it rained hard but it did stop for us to leave. Lots of hills again. Made the Spar at Bow before the rain started again.

Then our next disaster happened. We were on a nice 30 mph downhill when my pannier came off and lodged in my brake. Luckily it missed the spokes and we made Crediton (The Bikeshed) and our second bike shop. We managed to get the ripped material of the saddle bag out of the brake and repair the mangled pannier rack before carrying on.

Lots of hills before a welcome respite at Bradninch (*ski*) to admire a beautiful view of a local Latvian blonde. Spurred on by this sight we raced downhill to Cullompton, where we saw deer and impala of all things in the grounds of some fancy estate. I used to live in Kenya where impala were as common as sparrows in the game parks but you hardly expect to see them in a rain-soaked field in Devon! I spent the next half hour watching out for lions. Well, you never know do you?

We headed on for a bit before Derek managed to find a river to watch trout in and I laughed 'cos at last something went wrong with Derek's bike as one of his panniers snapped. 'Bicycle repair man' quickly sorted the problem though and on we went. Had a quick pub stop; coke and crisps, before gingerly getting back in the saddle.

Riding on we discovered Somerset (a bit like John Simpson liberating Kabul back in 2001). Somerset is an old English name although ancient humans have lived here since Paleolithic times.

Being a Welshman whose often ribbed by his English friends about living in caves it was interesting to learn of the bones found in Cheddar Gorge of a bloke that dated back to 12,000 BC. Some caves, like Wookey Hole, have even had people living in them until fairly modern times. Maybe they should twin with Blaencwm? Oops, just kidding!

'Thinking We're Almost At Glastonbury'

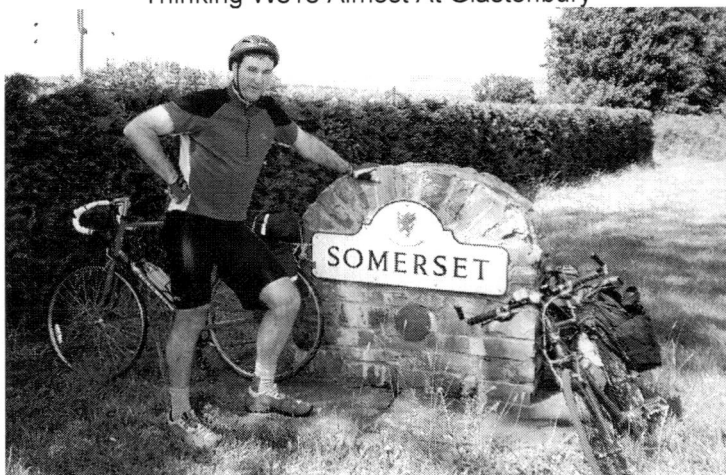

One of many county signposts

28

We pushed on and made it to Wellington. The town that gave its name to the first Duke of Wellington; Arthur Wellesley, who is commemorated by the nearby Wellington Monument. We didn't bother to take a photo 'cos we were knackered and didn't want to be seen glamorising war. Although thinking back maybe we should have because while the Iron Duke wasn't much of a Prime Minister his battle record was incredible. He fought in sixty battles and defeated Napoleon at Waterloo of course. In fact he is regarded as one of the greatest defensive commanders of all time, and many of his tactics and battle plans are still studied in military academies around the world today.

Derek asked how far we had to go.

'Nearly there mate, I reckon about nine or ten miles left today,' I cheerfully replied.

'Great stuff. I'm starting to struggle a bit now,' said the super fit Derek.

'Is Glastonbury next to Taunton then Dave?'

'Yeh buttie. It must be,' I hesitated. 'Oh shit,' I said, under my breath.

So, on we pedalled for about seven miles until we by-passed Taunton at rush hour with added road works and angry car drivers (not nice) and then we realised I'd miscalculated the distance somewhere and we were still ten miles short of our destination - oops.

'Are you sure?' asked Derek.

'Yeh, of course it is. Must be a mile or so further that's all...'

'You're lying aren't you?' said Derek.

'Yeh I am.'

We kept going with sore bum, sore legs, sore wrists, sore bits and bobs and finally crawled into Glastonbury on our hands and pedals having covered an amazing seventy-nine miles! My best ever.

It's a funny old place Glastonbury. Famous these days for the music festival, unusually high rainfall in June and rich kids playing in the mud.

Years ago it was an important Pagan site but like many places in Europe the Christians hijacked the myths and legends and turned them all religious.

The town today is a mish-mash of arty-farty candle and crystal shops, yoga classes and a kind of weird hippy hangout for people who use the word 'creative' or 'spiritual' a lot in conversation, put their hair into dreadlocks and have tattoos of angels drawn all over their breasts.

The Glastonbury Tor and Abbey ruins are worth seeing though. There is a lot of argument over these things but many claim Glastonbury Abbey is King Arthur's final resting place. Welshmen think it's Caerleon in south Wales of course.

We had a quick wash at the King William Inn, a pint of Stella, scampi and chips and then we partied like there was no tomorrow at a pagan, full moon, incensed-filled, open air, nightclub-in-a-field rave with 1000 naked virgins... and then I was woken up by 'Bob the builder' (local lad) who'd noticed we'd both fallen asleep leaning on the bar. Had a little chat where he assured us we'd never make it over the

Mendips. His actual words were 'The Wells hill will kill you!' Great news we thought. Don't you just love local knowledge like that! Can't wait!

I had to top-up my mobile credit so went for a walk and phoned Sue. She asked if I was tired but I was too tired to reply.

'Hello? Are you still there?'

'Night love, zzzzzz.'

I returned to the pub, had another pint of Stella, played some pool and then grabbed a chilli burger and chips in order to try to make my belly even bigger.

Then I went to bed to cry myself to sleep.

Cycling Stats

Start: 7:00am
Distance: 79.06 miles
Total Distance: 200.10 miles
Average Speed: 12.3 mph
Fastest Speed: 38.2 mph
Cycling Time: 6 hrs 25 mins
Finish: 6:30pm
Beers: 3

Day Four
Tuesday 5th July 2005
Glastonbury to Gloucester

We rose quite early but there was no sign of our bikes and everything in the building was locked up tighter than a duck's bottom in a drakes-only prison for wayward waterfowl. Was thinking of ringing Captain Kirk to scan for life forms when the pub landlady finally got up and made us a nice breakie.

We said our hearty goodbyes, left the sleepy, little, hippy village of Glastonbury - the place where one thousand BBC journalists and hangers-on suddenly descend, once a year, and demand a 5 star hotel when the music festival is in town, and tried not to get lost.

On the bikes again and feeling a bit better although the legs are starting to know what sore is now. Made good time to Wells, the home of the posh cathedral which is the seat of the Bishop of Bath and Wells. A name I can't take seriously after Black Adder's baby-eating bishop.

The present building dates from 1175 to 1490, but an earlier church was built on the site in 705. The architecture is entirely Gothic and mostly in a single style, which is kinda cool as old religious buildings go.

We stopped to take some pictures of the big church but then it started raining - serves me right for being a lapsed Buddhist I thought.

Then it rained some more. Then it really rained. Then it got cold, very cold. In fact, not to put to fine a point on it, it pissed down!

'Munching On Something Again'

Wells Cathedral in the rain - still glorious!

We somehow managed to get lost and went the wrong way out of Wells (I blame Derek, his huge pile of maps and his Geography degree) and eventually found a very big hill in the rain to cycle up. I immediately started feeling ill and my dodgy chest (think previous double pneumonia and five days in hospital) began to play up.

We cycled on, up the Mendips (which sound like they should really be downhill) until eventually we couldn't see anymore, such was the strength of the horizontal rain that misted Derek's glasses up and made me forget about rip-off Britain and concentrate my moans and groans on the great British summer weather instead.

We stopped for a brief respite in a Co-op on top of the hill and got some more Lucozade and chocolate such was our addiction to glucose by this stage.

I'd read somewhere about professional cyclists stuffing newspaper down their jumpers to insulate them against the cold and so wandered over to the kindly shop staff to ask if they could give us an old copy of yesterday's local paper in order to save our lives.

'No, you'll have to buy one if you want one!' a sullen woman with a face like a slapped kipper replied.

'Ahh! I hate rip-off Britain!' I cried.

I pinched two anyway and ran out of the shop like a kid from Grange Hill. Like hell were they going to chase us in that rain!

So, we had our emergency hi-tech chest warmers and quickly stuffed the newspapers down our fronts to prevent pneumonia. I could see the headline now - 'The Somerset Gazette saves another life in charity horror ride!' Not likely to have happened with the Ponty Observer that's for sure – no news in it!

We sped downhill into Bath (looking like we'd just had one) but couldn't find a launderette to dry out. We settled for a trendy Jazz Cafe instead and joined the well-to-do lunchtime yuppies for a nice, hot beans on toast with lashings of hot tea.

We were both dripping wet so I headed for the bathroom (sorry restroom) to try to use the hand dryer on my sodden clothes. For some reason I got really funny looks from a local man who wondered why I was directing hot air from the hand dryers down my cycling shorts, but to be honest at this point I was beyond caring!

The very young, but lovely, shop owner gave us directions out of town (even braving the rain himself to walk down the street with us to point to the main road) and we managed to find lots more hills (Derek was happy again), country lanes and very posh houses as the 'Bike Britain' route came into it's own and we soon became sopping in Sopworth.

We rode on until Derek spotted a Post Office. He decided he wanted to get a stamp on our sopping wet, sodding Land's End passports. I was dubious, fearing if we didn't get out of this county soon we might drown but we were so glad we did stop.

On our journey we met lots of people, some nice, some not so nice. And as the saying goes 'It takes all sorts'. Well, in a little village called Luckington our luck changed. We met a fantastic guy - John Sykes, who runs the Post Office there. He welcomed us in out of the rain, gave us directions to the biggest downhill in Gloucestershire, between Cockadilly and Frocester, which was very nice after all the climbs. He also gave us free drinks (Red Bull) and some bars of Turkish Delight. All we can do is say thank you John very much!

So suitably recharged we pushed on. We found the big downhill John had pointed us towards but the road was very wet and greasy. Like the true gentleman I am (and complete coward) I let Derek the nutter go first.

All I heard was a scream through the rain...

Derek nearly lost it at about 40 mph and almost got creamed by a lorry as he skidded across the road and just avoided the traffic coming uphill at us. I think he must have missed the great views of the Severn Valley that I saw as his life flashed before him.

Our final ride into Gloucester town was flat and we were still on target for fourteen days with another sixty-nine miles knocked off the total.

We tried a few B&Bs but again found no room at the inn. Eventually we managed to get some grumpy old bat to give us a room in a crap pub in the centre of town for £30 a night (I shouted again, you can guess what).

We dressed the room's radiators with our soaking wet clothes and put on our very damp, dry clothes (shorts, t-shirt and flip-flops) and ventured out onto the streets of Gloucester. I rang my dad to see how he was feeling and then spoke to Sue too. Eve was playing up again...

Gloucester lies close to the Welsh border, and River Severn. It is a cathedral city, and was founded in AD 97 by the Romans, although many references to the settlement were made in various Welsh language accounts of the early rulers of Britain.

The pub we were staying at was a bit of a building site so I was thinking of making a joke about Fred West but decided against it and instead informed Derek that Simon Pegg of 'Shaun of the Dead' fame came from Gloucester. Yeh, much safer.

None of this mattered much to us though as we searched for a decent chippy. We ate our pie and chips while arguing about the *English* Olympic bid with a local drunk in the Chinese takeaway. I confidently predicted that London would never get it in a million years! And even if they did it would be crap. I'm very perceptive like that.

Suitably satiated with a couple of thousand kilojoules of carbohydrates we decided to have a couple of quiet pints in the hotel. Why risk getting into any further discussions about how much an Olympic bribe costs these days?

We talked to a nice young lad behind the bar but the night was ruined by a complete dick from Torquay who started insulting the Welsh to try to get a rise from us. I was about five seconds away from starting some corrective dental work when Derek sensed the tension and dragged me away. Guess he didn't fancy being homeless on the damp streets of Gloucester.

Late getting to bed (about midnight) but neither of us could sleep much due to the 'Turkish bath' atmosphere our drying clothes created, the drunken idiots in the street and the noisy seagulls outside - Britain on a Tuesday eh! Don't you just love it.

Cycling Stats

Start: 9:30am
Distance: 69.37 miles
Total Distance: 269.47 miles
Average Speed: 11.0 mph
Fastest Speed: 34.5 mph
Cycling Time: 6 hrs 15 mins
Finish: 7:15pm
Beers: 3

Day Five
Wednesday 6th July 2005
Gloucester to Church Stretton

Awake at five o'clock in the morning to the sound of seagulls playing 'Pass the Sprat' or something on the roof above our heads. Tried to close the curtains to shut out the light but just succeeded in breaking the window instead. Oops. I think it's a listed building as well.

Eventually got up at 7:30am for breakfast, my chest feels terrible, but we manage to pack and get on the road again by 8:30am.

Things are going well, we're speeding along when disaster strikes again about three miles outside Gloucester. Derek scratches his head only to notice that he can. As in, he doesn't have his helmet on.

'Bollocks, that was a new helmet, I'm going back,' he says.

'Ah leave it, we've come this far without falling off,' I helpfully point out.

Back he goes to the hotel hoping they haven't discovered the broken window yet. In true explorer spirit, like Shackleton before me, I push on alone into a strong headwind. As I point out to Derek, he's much fitter than me and it'll give him a challenge to try and catch up with me.

We're reunited at the M50 junction near Redmarley and we finally reach Ledbury, which looks like a really nice place, by break time. We re-stock with eight Lucozades and a 10-pack of KitKat (I kid you not!) and it all comes to a massive 69p (cheers Lucozade).

After a day of colonic irrigation yesterday (no mudguards, slight oversight on my part) my piles are back with a vengeance and we find a really nice uphill section at Bromyard on the supposedly flattest day of the ride. Nice views of Hay Bluff in the distance which brings home the realisation just how far we still have to go seeing as we're only just level with the southern most tip of mid Wales!

Downhill to Tenbury Wells and the River Teme which Derek is particularly fond of being a world-class fisherman as well as an excellent cyclist. The River Teme rises in mid Wales and flows across the border into England before reaching the fab town of Ludlow. It then continues to the north of Tenbury Wells where it joins the River Severn, to the south of Worcester. Picturesque, attractive and fast flowing in parts this river is truly spectacular. Derek tells me all about the fish.

'It's got Barbel, Chub, Bream, Grayling, Perch and Eels,' he points out.

'I thought they wrote My Beloved Monster,' I say.

While I rest up by the river, nurse my piles and think of Steve Buscemi in 'Things To Do In Denver When Your Dead' Derek strolls into town. He soon returns with a giant punnet of strawberries and proceeds to tell tales of woe about when he used to pick them. Suffice to say 'manure', 'Moroccans' and 'shared toilet facilities' don't do much to inspire the greatest health and hygiene standards on British fruit-picking farms.

He's now complaining I'm ahead of him on the diary writing but I quickly remind him that I didn't have to cycle back to Gloucester did I (tee hee).

The two of us are coughing in stereo now as the lurgies bed in so there's nothing for it but to find more hills to cycle up. We do find more hills and then disaster - my pile of shite Dawes Discovery 701 breaks a spoke and my pannier rack snaps!

'Wasn't the best purchase Dave was it?' Derek helpfully points out.

'Aye, I know. But in fairness to me I did ask them if these racing wheels would hold my weight (100kg at time of starting the ride) plus some panniers and they assured me yes they'd be fine,' I reply.

'Think they were lying.'

'Yeh, they were. Bastards!'

We now have a race against the clock. It's two miles to Ludlow and the shops are shutting in ten minutes! Feel like I'm on a TV game show or something. But somehow with every bit of bad luck that gets thrown at us we also get blessed with a bit of good fortune too. Is that bikers karma or something I wonder?

Anyway, we stop at a pet shop to ask if there are any bike shops in town and are told no. But, the very attractive young girl says, 'Funny you should be looking for a bike shop as that's what this shop used to be and my dad might be able to help.' Off she goes and a few minutes later we find the only man alive in England who can actually make a spoke! Start counting the bike shops again...

Fred of CWA Cycles actually made us one from scratch! What a guy! The fact it was the wrong size and he charged me £5.50 is irrelevant - I was happy in my ignorance and sang his praises to all who'd listen until the next spoke broke.

We left Ludlow as we were men on a mission and wanted to get as far up the road as we could. This was a shame though as Ludlow is a wonderful town. It's got a cool castle, about 500 listed buildings and the best real ale for miles around!

Ludlow is in Shropshire, our next county, and has a fascinating history. The town played a big role in local, regional and national conflicts such as the Owain Glyndŵr rebellion, the Wars of the Roses and the English Civil War. Ludlow was also a temporary home to several holders of the title Prince of Wales, including King Edward IV and Arthur Tudor, who died there in 1502.

Now for more of that lady luck... the rain was followed by a headwind. There was no way we'd make Shrewsbury so we just pushed on until we got knackered. We kept cycling, head down, arse up, as far as the wind would allow us.

Over hydrated again thanks to all the Lucozade, I stopped to release some excess liquid from my bladder at a seemingly deserted lay-by just as a bus pulled in. The poor, eighty year old lady looked like she'd had a heart attack as she was escorted away. Not sure why though as the constant cold and rain, the six hours or more a day in the saddle was making my normally proud old boy resemble a shrivelled and shrunken salami!

Not long after my flashing experience the weather seemed to draw us into a place called Church Stretton that reminded me of the Stepford Wives. It was very weird and creepy. We cycled past Craven Arms, then started seeing strange signs where all the place names looked the same, we saw signs to places like Strefford, Little Stretton, Ticklerton, All Stretton, Minton etc.

'Hey Derek, this place is like Midsummer Murders,' I called through the hail.

'What?'

'You know, little so-and-so, upper so-and-so, middle so-and-so, church so-and-so...'

'I think the rain is playing tricks with your mind Dave.'

'Maybe. Well as long as we don't happen upon a quaint little village with lots of posh people going to fetes with jam and amateur dramatics I'll be fine.'

We'd cycled twelve miles into a rain-filled headwind when we finally made Little Stretton and decided enough was enough. We found a guesthouse with ponds outside filled with huge carp. There was a poster on the wall of the passage. Something about a summer fete. I gulped but Derek was happy again because he could look at fish. I tried to phone home but there was no mobile coverage.

'Maybe we're between two valleys and there are no masts,' said Derek.

'Maybe they've cut the lines before the zombies are unleashed,' I replied.

We went out for some food. Everyone smiled but there was still no mobile reception. Would we ever leave this nice place? It was like a moonie convention and the place was full of unsuspecting mountain bikers - very disconcerting.

We had a sweet and sour chicken, with half and half (short on the rice though) and a Guinness in a local pub which was absolutely packed when we arrived but in true Stepford Wives fashion the place was deserted five minutes after the last fork was put down on a plate. I was starting to get the shivers - very Scooby Doo. Then I noticed a flyer on the next table. Something about the local acting troupe putting on a performance of Macbeth.

Afraid we'd be kidnapped by aliens with anal probes we went home. Pleased we'd covered a very hard sixty-five miles on what should have been an easy section but annoyed with ourselves for falling behind our schedule. The first real set back of the trip.

Cycling Stats

Start: 8:30am
Distance: 65.78 miles
Total Distance: 335.25 miles
Average Speed: 10.4 mph
Fastest Speed: 31.7 mph
Cycling Time: 6 hrs 19 mins
Finish: 7:15pm
Beers: 2

Day Six
Thursday 7th July 2005
Church Stretton to Speke

First good nights sleep on the whole trip so far - we were zonked until 6:30am. Maybe the wives drugged us I suggested to Derek.

Measly breakfast (with no pork sausages - was this another sign?) and we were on our way. Missing Sue and Eve lots today and fed up with yesterday having missed our distance goal. Still no mobile reception to ring home, but soon realised why when we heard the news later that evening. Although why neither of our mobiles worked the previous night we can't explain. Unless of course you think Alex Jones of Info Wars is sane and that all conspiracy theories are actually true.

Taken from the history.co.uk website:

In London, at 8.50am three bombs exploded simultaneously, destroying sections of three different London Underground trains. One was detonated just outside Liverpool Street station, the other outside Edgware Road and the third between Kings Cross and Russell Square. Around an hour later at 9.50am there was an explosion on the top level of a double-decker bus in Tavistock Square near Kings Cross, caused by a similar device to the ones used on the underground.

The explosions left 52 innocent people dead and over 700 injured. Chaos erupted across the capital, echoing the horrific terrorist attacks faced by New York four years before, on 11 September 2001. The worst bombing in London since WWII, it brought the city's public transport network to a standstill.

In the immediate aftermath of the bombings victims on the tube used fire extinguishers to break down train doors. Passengers on the Piccadilly line train between King's Cross to Russell Square who were able to walk felt their way in the darkness down the length of the tunnel back to ground level. The following day the Metropolitan Police stated that it could not be ruled out that the attacks were 'the result of suicide bombings'.

The bombers were later confirmed to be Muslims. 30 year old Mohammad Sidique Khan, 24 year old Shehzad Tanweer, 19 year old Germaine Lindsay and 18 year old Hasib Hussain. Following the events of 7/7 all four bombers were found to be British citizens said to be leading normal every day lives, including Khan who was a teaching assistant in his native Beeston, Leeds.

Two of the bombers also resided in North Yorkshire near to where the organic peroxide based devices were later found to have been constructed. On 12 July police discovered much of the bombing equipment still in tact in a rented flat in the Hyde Park area of Leeds.

Khan, Tanweer and Hussain were all of Pakistani descent and Jamaican-born Germaine Lindsay of Huddersfield, West Yorkshire, was a convert to Islam. The investigation into the bombings found that both Mohammad Sidique Khan and Shehzad Tanweer had previously spent several months in Pakistan where it is very likely that they were in contact with Al-Qaeda and went through extensive extremist training.

The 7/7 bombings were subsequently linked with the attempted bombings of 21 July 2005. Only two weeks after the initial attacks, failed devices were found in similar locations; one on a double-decker bus and three others on trains on the London Underground. There was some speculation that the attacks on 21 July were the work of the same Islamist cell, although another theory is that the would-be bombers were simply copycats.

When the verdict of the inquests into 7/7 was released in May 2011, it was welcomed by the victims' families, but some said that they still feel there should be a full inquiry into the bombings. Despite the fact the Prime Minister at the time, Tony Blair, promised that all evidence would be published, this has yet to happen.

As with the terrible events of 9/11, there are conspiracy theories surrounding the events of that day, including so called 'co-incidences'. One example concerns British crisis management specialist Peter Power, who on that very day had planned a crisis management simulation drill.

In the immediate aftermath of the attacks candlelit vigils were held in the capital and the Union flag was flown at half mast in remembrance of those who died. In 2009, the Prince of Wales paid tribute to the bravery of the bereaved families and survivors of the bombings as he unveiled a memorial in Hyde

Park dedicated to the 52 people who died on 7 July 2005.

'The Romans Couldn't Beat Us, So Neither Will The Muslims!'

Roman clock, Whitchurch

We cycled into Shrewsbury at nine o'clock, and tried two more bike shops (neither of them any good). Pee'd off with my bike big time now. Cycled on to Wem, where we found the best bike shop in Britain (yet another spoke had broken on my brand new bike by this time!). Mark Lancaster of Jack

Davies Cycles fixed them for free, which restored our faith in humanity again.

Shrewsbury is a pleasant, medieval, market town with over 600 listed buildings and a nice castle. I would have liked to have stayed last night if the elements weren't against us as it's the birthplace of one of my heroes, Charles Darwin, who along with Welshman Alfred Russel Wallace, was the discoverer of evolution, but time was against us and so we had to push on.

Next we cycled on to Whitchurch, which is two miles east of the Welsh border, in the Marches. Nothing to do with Royal Marines yomping about the place the term 'marches' denotes a precisely defined territory, the marches between England and the Principality of Wales, in which Marcher lords had specific rights, like a marquis in France.

Whitchurch (or White Church) was originally a Roman settlement founded around AD 52 or 70, and called Mediolanum, which translates as Midfield. I took a few photos, especially of the lovely Roman clock, as the sun came out for once.

Pedalling on we entered the county of Cheshire, home of Lewis Carroll (hence the Cheshire Cat). We carried on through Delemere Forest (a lovely lake with ducks for me and fish for Derek to look at) until possibly the worst part of the trip...

Yep, hell on earth - Runcorn! What a shithole! Incredibly, people actually live here! Sorry folks, but they do! OK, time out, we can't all live in a five-bed mansion set in beautiful rolling countryside but there must be more to life than this?

We cycled on before we got sucked into a dystopian *Blade Runner*-type future and nearly got mowed down by various lorries, vans, cars and trucks before having to cross a nightmare road bridge and then on to John Lennon Airport.

Still in one piece our nerves were calmed when we found Speke, which in contrast is quite nice, and very flat. I know what you're thinking. Why on earth did we detour here? Well, Derek's bingo hall manager mate Sean lives here. Why else?

We found his house but he was still at work. It didn't matter though as we got let in by a friendly neighbour and had a bath each. That's each, not together, by the way.

While Derek played with his rubber duck I rang Sue and it was only then that we heard about the London bombings. Having grown up in the seventies and eighties with the ever-present threat of the IRA it was slightly déjà vu but none the less very disturbing.

When Sean came home from work he took us out for a magical mystery tour of Strawberry Fields, the name of a Salvation Army children's home just around the corner from John Lennon's childhood home in Woolton, a suburb of Liverpool, and we also saw Eleanor Rigby's grave. I was hoping he'd have some connection to Lucy in the Sky with Diamonds but you can't have everything I suppose. It was a bit surreal, but when in Rome...

Sean is a big Beatles fan and showed us some of the houses owned by The Beatles before we went for an expensive Chinese meal and a few beers. I have to say though being served a Chinese meal by a Chinese lad with a strong, scouser accent ranks up there with being one of the weirdest experiences of the trip. It just didn't sound right! Chinese people should have Welsh accents surely?

'Visiting Graveyards And Old Childrens Homes, At Night, In Liverpool'

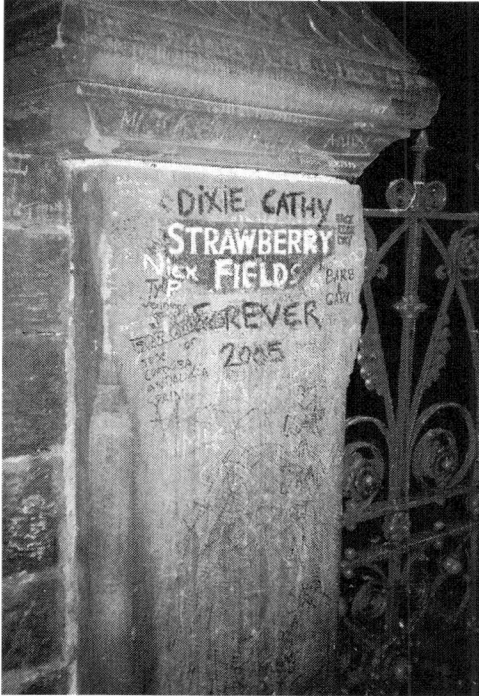

Strawberry Fields Forever

Feels good to be back on track after a hard seventy-six miles today and the low point yesterday. But when we think about the poor innocent victims of the Muslim terrorists living amongst us it puts into perspective the sore arse, tired legs and my constant moans and groans.

Cycling Stats

Start: 7:30am
Distance: 76.32 miles
Total Distance: 411.57 miles
Average Speed: 10.9 mph
Fastest Speed: 29.4 mph
Cycling Time: 6 hrs 58 mins
Finish: 8:00pm
Beers: 3

Day Seven
Friday 8th July 2005
Speke to Lancaster

Sue and Eve phoned at 6:50am. We talked about the evil bombers, the dead victims and how Islam seems to want to take over the world. A bit like Christianity I guess but not in a nice way. Then I noticed the Milo and Bella wallpaper in our room (Sean's kids) and thought about how the Teletubbies and Tweenies would probably be banned under Sharia Law. So too would singing and dancing and bright colours. I thought about how my father had fought the Muslim Brotherhood in Egypt during the 1950s. I thought about their motto 'Jihad is our way; death for the sake of Allah is our wish' and wondered why they couldn't just jump on a bike and go for a nice ride from Land's End to John o' Groats instead. If they did that they'd see how wonderful it is to live in a relatively, free country like the UK and also be too knackered to cause trouble!

Then I thought about my sore arse and aching legs again. And the fact that we still hadn't reached the halfway point in our pilgrimage.

So, not feeling great, with fatigue well and truly set in now off we set again with another punishing seventy miles to look forward to.

'Who's idea was this?' I asked.

'Yours, and I have the beer mat to prove it' said Derek grinning.

After yesterday's nightmare through Runcorn we were expecting the industrial north to engulf us, especially when we looked at the maps and saw a tangled web of spaghetti motorways and A roads but we were very pleasantly surprised.

We cycled along some lovely flat roads, there was no pollution and we had a great day as we headed through Huyton, Prescott, St Helens, two Eccleston's (via a free coke in the pub) and Leyland (home of the truck). The sun was shining, Derek found a canal for us to cycle along for a bit and then we saw the houses!

Being a rugby fan (Union and League) I confidently prophesied that these huge sprawling mansions with matching Range Rover, Ferrari and Lamborghini accessories must belong to the players of Warrington, St Helen's, Widnes etc. but then we realised we'd somehow strayed into millionaires row... ah, footballers. The real overpaid sportsmen of this unfair and unjust land.

The next half hour was spent with Derek silently listening to me quote Karl Marx and ranting about the *haves* (footballers) and *have-nots* (us two) while occasionally stopping to admire a property that would even make big-bosomed, property developer Sarah Beeny jealous. We were half hoping to spot some of the footballers wives too but then realised the shops were open so gave up on that idea.

We left Cheshire and entered Lancashire, famous for its red rose, battle with York and various food stuffs. There's black pudding, Chorley cakes, Eccles cakes, hotpot, Uncle Joe's Mint Balls (I'm not trying to be rude honest!), butter cake, faggots, oatcakes, cheeses and Ormskirk gingerbread for starters.

Next up was Preston and yet another bike shop (are you still counting?) where a very nice man fixed our bikes for free (to support our charity) and also gave us a free gear service (whatever that is?). Then on to Lancaster. We actually arrived early for once after a very pleasant sixty-two miles by 4:30pm.

Lancaster is one of the many places on our route that is first recorded in the Domesday Book, circa 1086. Loncastre, as it was known originates from 'Lon' (River Lune) and 'castre' (Latin for fort).

The Roman fort which stood on the hill where Lancaster Castle now stands dates back as early as the first Century AD, based on the Roman coin evidence.

Following the Norman conquest of England in 1066, Lancaster fell under the control of William I, and so like most of Britain, became French.

Lancaster Castle, partly built in the 13th Century and enlarged by Elizabeth I, stands on the site of a Roman garrison. It is well known as the site of the Pendle Witch Trials in 1612. It was said that the court based in the castle (the Lancaster Assizes) sentenced more people to be hanged than any other in the country, outside of London, earning Lancaster the nickname, 'the Hanging Town'.

'Best not hang around here too long,' I said to Derek.

'Shut up,' said Derek.

'Derek, All In Lancastrian Red, With His Trusty
One Litre Robinsons Squash Bottle'

Lancaster Castle (Red Rose)

Of course as all good history buffs know, the traditional emblem for the House of Lancaster is a red rose. The House of York on the other hand has a white rose. These names derive from the emblems of the Royal Duchies of Lancaster and York. The civil war that erupted over rival claims to the throne became known at the Wars of the Roses. Welshman Henry Tudor, (he was born in Pembroke Castle), a Lancastrian, defeated King Richard III, a Yorkist, at the battle of Bosworth Field on 22 August 1485. I'm just glad daffodils are mostly one colour.

We booked into a nice pub after getting no useful information from the tourist information office and had a bath and a pint of Black Sheep real ale to celebrate being back on track again.

We walked around the town, which was very nice, had a lovely fish and chips in the Littern Tree pub, a couple more pints and I phoned home to talk to mam and dad.

Sue rang and I said hello to Eve, who had stopped playing up for a minute. Just a minute though.

We did a bit of a mini pub crawl before going home to watch Christopher Lee and his third nipple fight James Bond to the death in Thailand. Big thanks to a local man in the pub (forgot to get his name) who did a whip round for us and raised a few quid for our cause.

Cycling Stats

Start: 8:00am
Distance: 62.12 miles
Total Distance: 473.69 miles
Average Speed: 10.7 mph
Fastest Speed: 29.4 mph
Cycling Time: 5 hrs 45 mins
Finish: 4:30pm
Beers: 4

Day Eight
Saturday 9th July 2005
Lancaster to Carlisle (over half way!)

Didn't get much sleep, very tired but up at 6:45am for a fantastic breakie - two eggs, two sausages, tomatoes, beans, bacon, black pudding, fried bread... (cue: Ken Owen, Ynysybwl RFC, pre-RWC Wales match, 1995).

On the road by 8:00am with a full belly and it wasn't long before we saw deer, heron, rabbits and plenty of raptors. Being a zoologist I was in hogs heaven but Derek was only interested in fish.

'Sunshine At Last, We Seek Shelter
From Useless Car Drivers'

Kendal Bridge

We made good speed to the town of Kendal in the beautiful county of Cumbria, an old Celtic kingdom. It has a nice bridge but far too many tourists who can't drive properly, especially when confronted by two Welsh cyclists minding their own business!

Kendal is best known for its Kendal mint cake of course, a glucose-based confectionery often used on mountaineering expeditions the world over (including Mount Everest and K2). The sweet also supplied one of my heroes; Ernest Shackleton, on his incredible 1914–17 Trans-Antarctic Expedition.

Derek and I couldn't pass up the chance to indulge either (we were still in the grips of Lucozade poisoning / addiction at this stage of the ride) and so we made a quick visit to the local shop for snacks and postcards.

We wrote our postcards in a park by the river and celebrated the fact that we had finally reached the halfway point! It was quite a feeling.

'Bloody hell only half way!' I moaned.

'Yep, all downhill from now,' added Derek.

'Really?' I asked.

'Well, after one of the biggest hills in the Lake District,' he said.

I won't repeat what I said.

We set off for Shap hill, enjoyed the lovely views and got sunburnt for the first time. Although steep, the hills we cycled over were no bigger than those around Brecon, so for once being Welsh had its advantages.

We stopped for a pint and some sandwiches in Shap town and then rode downhill to Penrith, yet another old Celtic town, where even more southern tourists can't drive to safe their lives!

'After Going Over The Big Hill'

Coke stop, Shap, Lake District

I've been to Penrith loads of times (usually the place we stop when driving back from Edinburgh after the Scotland v Wales Six Nations rugby international) and really like the town and the local people. We went to a crap outdoor shop then spotted a pub with a beer garden...

We talked to some nice Geordies about mountain biking across the hills. They were very helpful and told us a good ride was from West to East cross-country from Carlisle to Newcastle (maybe another time).

We cycled through nice rolling hills to Carlisle and arrived about 6:00pm, (sixty-nine miles all day) but due to recent floods there was very little room at the inn (again) and it took us over thirty minutes to finally find a B&B. At £25 each rip-off Britain was back to haunt us and I screamed again...

Carlisle is another Celtic town established by the Roman's to serve the forts on Hadrian's Wall.

It is a common misconception that Hadrian's Wall marks the boundary between England and Scotland. In fact Hadrian's Wall lies entirely within England - less than one kilometre south of the border in the west, but 110 kilometres south in the east.

'The Biggest Town In Cumbria, Last Stop Before Scotland'

Carlisle Town Centre

Got a meatball bap in the not very Celtic Subway and then we were out on the lash big time as it was Saturday night in Carlisle - hooray!

61

Managed a couple of pints in various smoky pubs that would let us in with shorts and flip-flops (our only change of clothes for two weeks) before getting fed up with the weird looks we were getting from the town's super-glamorous, dolly birds and dolly blokes.

Home via the chippie and Derek decided to sample some local delicacy, a deep-fried potato and onion ball in batter, while I went for the tried and tested pickled egg and chips. No prizes for guessing the glorious smell in the B&B Sunday morning.

Cycling Stats

Start: 8:00am
Distance: 69.67 miles
Total Distance: 543.36 miles
Average Speed: 10.6 mph
Fastest Speed: 33.9 mph
Cycling Time: 6 hrs 30 mins
Finish: 6:30pm
Beers: 3

Day Nine
Sunday 10th July 2005
Carlisle to Crawford (into our second country)

Up early but didn't get breakie 'till late. A slow start but we found a nice road out of Carlisle as we leave merry England behind.

'It Certainly Did'

Crossing the border at Gretna

We cross the border into Scotland and take a photo. Well, you've got to, haven't you? Then we get to Gretna and the blacksmiths where Derek decides he doesn't want to marry me after all! I'm very disappointed and after much persuasion, some flowers and a bended knee (probably cartilage from an old rugby injury) he finally agrees. Decide not to

63

tell Sue, because after all, our honeymoon was just one night away while me and Derek still have seven or eight days left together.

Find a great road straight north but then... yes you guessed it... disaster strikes again! My crappy Dawes bike snaps another spoke after just twenty miles cycling.

'Derek Says I Do, But I Forgot The Ring'

The Old Blacksmiths Shop, Gretna Green

We limped into Lockerbie, in Dumfries and Galloway, the town that came to international attention in December 1988 when the wreckage of Pan Am Flight 103 crashed there following a Syrian terrorist bomb aboard the flight. This very real disaster killed all 243 passengers and sixteen crew on board, as well as eleven more people on the ground. In case you're thinking I've got that wrong and it was Gaddafi, no I haven't, this is just our biased media reporting whatever the politicians tell them in order to make us OK with whatever war they fancy doing next. It wasn't anything to do with Libya but it was the Syrians, and probably the Iranians too.

Although famous now for all the wrong reasons Lockerbie has actually had a very interesting history. The site having existed since at least the days of Viking influence in the period around AD 900. The name (originally 'Loc-hard's by') means Lockard's Town in Old Norse. The presence of the remains of a Roman camp a mile to the west of the town suggests its origins are much earlier though.

'I think it's buggered for good this time,' I said.

'Yeh, can't cycle on with that,' confirmed Derek.

'Maybe there's a bike shop in town?' I wondered.

There wasn't.

It was also Sunday and the place was deserted. So, with no obvious help at hand we both just sat, dejected on the pavement.

It looked like our journey was finished. We thought about looking for a bus to a bigger town but even if we found one there'd only be a Sunday service. We wondered how much a taxi seventy-five miles north to Glasgow would cost.

'Shit, shit, shit!'

But just when we thought our trip might be over for good I flagged down a minibus of kindly forestry workers who were going to the beach with some tinnies.

'Hya. You're not passing Dumfries by any chance are you butties?'

I took off the offending back wheel and jumped aboard. Derek retired to the pub for the afternoon.

So with me and my wretched wheel and a bus full of Scottish nutters telling sick jokes about their town we headed west to Halfords where I soon discovered they didn't have spokes!

'Ahh!'

'What do you mean you can't fix a spoke? Is this a f***** bike shop or what?' I screamed at the poor lad who probably didn't want to work on a Sunday for minimum wage but thought what the hell, it's bound to be quiet...

Now, as I said before, we encountered many different people on our travels during the summer of 2005, some were downright rude, some were complete idiots but the vast majority were just wonderful. And both fate and the spirit of human kindness were definitely with us that day for a number of things happened in Dumfries and Galloway.

The first bit of good fortune was in Lockerbie, when I found the bus passing a Halfords on a deserted Sunday afternoon. The second thing was fate. I had the offending wheel in my hand and was after a spoke repair or re-fit, but little did I realise until I got back to Lockerbie that I'd somehow managed to lose my quick-release axle. I must have left it on the seat next to me on the minibus with the drunken forestry workers. So, if I had managed to get the spoke fixed I would have returned to Lockerbie without any means of attaching the wheel back on the bike!

So just as well I didn't. Instead I bought a new wheel to fit, which of course came with a new axle or spindle. I was about to shout something about rip-off Britain when I was told it was £34 but resisted the temptation such was my joy at finding a replacement wheel. I just hoped it would fit through my brake calipers because although it was the right circumference it looked mighty wide to me.

Now the third thing that happened to me was while I queued to pay for my spare wheel. I started chatting to this guy next to me and told him about our journey so far and the current mishap. I also asked if he knew of a bus stop nearby or where I might try and thumb a lift back.

'Ah, doubt you'll find a bus today,' he said.

'Oh dear. What about a taxi?' I asked.

'Too far and so very expensive. Come with me mate, I'm going that way.'

He wasn't. In fact he was going in completely the opposite direction!

So, this very kind man indeed offered me a lift (two wheel's and all) – twenty-eight miles out of his way! A grand gesture by a fellow Celt that probably saved our journey! What can you say? Cheers!!!

The man drove very fast. I got dropped off back in Lockerbie and bicycle repair man (Derek) made good the new wheel and inner tube in the Bluebell beer garden while we were watched by the South Sea Islander owner with a funny, pink haircut and a high pitched voice. Say no more.

So soon we were off again, albeit three hours late...

Deserted roads were followed by more deserted roads, on and on we went, this was real Doug McClure country! I half expected to be fighting off Velociraptors but somehow we clocked up a few miles.

'Ten Four Good Buddie'

Truck stop, Crawford

Eventually we stopped for some lovely sandwiches and chips at a good pub in the Scottish outback (at Beattock) run by some nice scousers on holiday. Stomachs full we headed straight back out into a headwind that saw us pedalling to stand still (like in the U2 song).

Suitably demoralised we decided there was nothing for it but to stop at Crawford - a truckers stop - where we booked a B&B&evening meal. We had no idea where we were but did enjoy a great three-course meal - melon starters, fish, chips and vegetables main course, with tumps of apple crumble for afters, just like my Nan used to make.

We went to the bar for a couple of pints, hoping to join in with the truckers banter about 'nice beavers' and looked forward to singing the chorus to 'I like to truck' but found the lorry drivers there mostly miserable, fat old gits that liked to murder rabbits and hedgehogs. Bad karma hey.

'Red Sky At Night Truckers Delight'

Our most eventful day so far...

We retired to bed after a miserable fifty-six miles (our worst day, mileage-wise, although probably our most eventful of the whole trip) but not before I took a photo of the stunning sunset. A fabulous red sky about 10:30pm at night.

Cycling Stats

Start: 8:45am
Distance: 56.09 miles
Total Distance: 599.45 miles
Average Speed: 10.5 mph
Fastest Speed: 23.3 mph
Cycling Time: 5 hrs 18 mins
Finish: 7:00pm
Beers: 2

Day Ten
Monday 11th July 2005
Crawford to Tarbet

Early rise, big greasy breakie as you'd expect for a truck stop (although not up to the Albion Kebab House, Cilfynydd, standard).

A beautiful morning, very cold, but clear blue skies - just magnificent. We were on the road by 6:35am and made great progress.

There were oystercatchers, lapwings, meadow pipits and rabbits everywhere.

'A veritable feast of Scottish fauna!' I exclaimed.

'Have you been on the diesel fumes again Dave?' replied Derek.

Quite a few hills to Douglas but about ten miles outside Glasgow we had great views down into the city and this really cheered us up. We cycle on, through Hamilton, and down into the city. I think it was about here that a local bus nearly creamed us both. I shouted some encouragement at the driver and beckoned him to vacate his comfy seat behind the wheel and engage in some polite fisticuffs with me but he declined and carried on his important council-sponsored quest to find more cyclists to murder.

We stopped at some traffic lights and I pointed out the signpost to the Gorbals. I told Derek about my great uncle (who was 6ft 4in, ex-miner, soldier, great rugby player and one tough bastard) who'd told me it was a bit 'rough' there when he'd visited with a squaddie friend in the fifties.

The Gorbals is an area of Glasgow on the south bank of the River Clyde. By the late 19th Century it became widely known as a dangerous slum with plenty of drunkenness, violence and crime. We hoped to blend in and move swiftly through but probably stood out like two southern nancys in Lycra with bikes that the scrappies would give a few bob for.

As we nervously waited for the lights to change a blue, soft-top Saab with the roof down, white leather seats and a page three stunner pulled out in front of us. She played with her hair for a bit, checked her perfect complexion in the mirror then adjusted the collar on her Prada blouse and sped off.

'Guess it's been redeveloped a bit nowadays,' I said.

Finally into one of my favourite UK cities - Glasgow. Where the people are awesome, as long as you're not wearing green and white hoops (Derek), or sky blue (me).

Glasgow is actually the largest city in Scotland, and the third largest in the UK (after London and Birmingham). It grew from a small rural settlement on the River Clyde to become the largest seaport in Britain. With the onset of the Industrial Revolution, the population and economy of Glasgow and the surrounding region expanded rapidly to become one of the world's pre-eminent centres of chemicals, textiles and engineering; most notably in the shipbuilding and marine engineering industries.

We'd covered thirty miles by 10:00am - the best ever - so decided we'd earned a stop. We had a coke and chatted to some locals who showed us the next bike shop on our tour of the bike shops of Britain and I had my spoke done on my spare wheel (I was carrying this strapped to the back of my panniers by now) for 60p. I didn't say a word.

Out of town we pushed on to Dumbarton and saw a Taff Trail ride-a-like which prevented heavy lorries from Crawford murdering us on the main road. We saw a few *Rab C Nesbit*-type women in the Alexandria Co-op as we re-stocked our Lucozades and laughed at the rows of Staff dogs all neatly lined up outside while the tattooed, obese and frankly quite scary women took it in turns to go in and buy cider and fags. Sheer class!

'Finally, Sunshine, Scotland And Stunning Scenery'

Loch Lomond

Finally we made the stunning Loch Lomond and had a pint of shandy at Duck Pool (the dearest pint in Britain according to Derek). It was very sunny again by now so we sat in the shade and gazed at the freezing cold water that was inviting us in! It was very tempting but as we were super-professional athletes we resisted. We wanted to stay here but had to push on to Tarbet to make up our distance for the day.

We arrived after six o'clock and found all the B&B's were full of bloody tourists on coach trips. We eventually found one on a hill with great views of the Loch run by a very nice Austrian lady (Mrs Mary McDonald) who even left chocolates on our pillows (don't tell Derek though 'cos I ate them before he saw them).

We went out to the 'church' for a few pints (a Bar & Restaurant that's been converted from an old church) and a rip-off Britain meal of bangers and mash for £8. Then into the Tarbet Hotel for a game of pool to avoid the Scottish dancers who seem to be stuck in a time warp as I'm sure I saw them about fourteen years earlier when I last stayed here with Sue and Greg before we headed over the sea to Skye to look for otters and Ian Anderson from Jethro Tull.

Suitably pleased with ourselves after falling behind in Crawford we were now back on track and my cheap Halfords wheel was working perfectly – bloody typical!

We leaned on the fence of a jetty and cast our gaze across the tranquil waters as the sun was setting. A truly beautiful spot where we stared lovingly into each others eyes for a few seconds before I fell about laughing as Derek discovered what giant horseflies and a million midge bites feel like. We'd heard horror stories about the summer insects here but to be honest they didn't seem to like the taste of me at all. Ah well.

A great day of cycling and we'd covered nearly eighty-two miles!

Cycling Stats

Start: 6:35am
Distance: 81.87 miles
Total Distance: 681.32 miles
Average Speed: 11.0 mph
Fastest Speed: 27.6 mph
Cycling Time: 7 hrs 26 mins
Finish: 6:20pm
Beers: 3

Day Eleven
Tuesday 12th July 2005
Tarbet to Fort William

An early-ish breakfast and on the road again by 8:15am. The road surface was terrible, there were buses, lorries and caravans all trying to drive as close to us as possible and we also had to cycle into numerous headwinds as we past lots of big Ben's and many, mighty Munro's.

The scenery was beautiful though, great for walking but it was very hard cycling into a wind like this. We managed to get up the hills OK but it was an absolute nightmare pedalling downhill against the wind. The wind seemed to be swirling around the mountains so we found ourselves permanently in our lowest gear, just to keep moving! Without doubt the worst winds of the trip that resulted in many long, hard slogs downhill believe it or not. We even stopped halfway down one hill to rest. Totally soul-destroying man!

Did eventually get some speed up as we passed some road works and weaved in and out of the cars at traffic lights (don't you just hate it when you're driving and bikes do that?).

Eventually made it to Glencoe completely knackered. Replenished fluids (yeh, you guessed it, more Lucozade) and sat by a stunning loch watching seagulls drop crabs onto the stones from a pre-determined height. Too low and the crabs' shells wouldn't crack, too high and another seagull might fly in and claim your prize. It took me back to my optimal foraging essays and talk of evolutionary stable strategies at Cardiff University - amazing to see it live!

I explained this to Derek.

'You're weird,' said Derek.

Pushed on to Fort William and the welcome sight of a thousand B&B signs... So how come we picked the duff one?

'Resting On A Downhill Stretch Due To The Swirling Winds'

Stunning Scottish Highlands

Fort William is a major tourist centre for hillwalking and climbing due to its proximity to Ben Nevis and many other Munro mountains. It first got its name from William of Orange, before going through various name changes; Maryburgh, Gordonsburgh and Duncansburgh before once more returning to Fort William after Prince William, Duke of Cumberland; known to some Scots as 'Butcher Cumberland' because of his putting down the Jacobite Rising at the Battle of Culloden in 1746. Gaelic speakers want to change the name to something more fitting but it hasn't happened yet.

I like Fort William. There is a weird familiarity about the place. I've been there quite a few times but it always feels like it's just down the road from home rather than the opposite end of the country. Strange but true.

With a good seventy miles under our lycra it was out for a few well deserved pints at the Nevis pub where everyone wants the window seat, followed by the Grub & Gruel which was full of tourists.

We were soon starving but couldn't find a curry house or even a chip shop open as the weird local council had made them shut early for some reason. The night ended with us sharing half a bar of Snickers (Marathon to us oldies) for supper.

Cycling Stats

Start: 8:15am
Distance: 70.11 miles
Total Distance: 751.43 miles
Average Speed: 10.5 mph
Fastest Speed: 30.1 mph
Cycling Time: 6 hrs 40 mins
Finish: 6:15pm
Beers: 4

Day Twelve
Wednesday 13th July 2005
Fort William to Dingwall

No early breakie (the lazy woman didn't get up) so we help ourselves to a quick bowl of cereal, and a couple of apples and bananas. We also stuff a few down the shorts to make us feel like real men again after all the genital shrinkage of the last few days and head off early.

For once the wind is with us (as is the drizzle). We glide effortlessly past loch after loch, through glade after glade... OK, enough of that.

We reach nearly 400 mph at some points. Alright, that was the RAF Tornados practicing their bombing of Muslim countries but we did go very fast.

We stop for breakie at the Spean Bridge Hotel - a lovely place but rip-off Britain is back on our cases and we get charged £6 for hardly anything at all to eat.

On to Fort Augustus where tourists (who look like Yanks, all kitted out in white socks and sandals, M&S shorts, massive SLR cameras and baseball caps) queue up to watch boats go through the Caledonian lock - strange people - have they never seen a lock before? They should visit Risca, there's fourteen of the buggers there!

Then it's on to the world-renowned Loch Ness but the monster appears to be in hiding or else she's just shy. The famous freshwater loch is very large, very deep (over 750 feet) and is almost twenty-three miles long so there is plenty of room to disappear I guess.

In fact Loch Ness is the second largest Scottish loch by surface area after Loch Lomond, but due to its great depth, it is the largest by volume in the British Isles. It is the second deepest loch in Scotland after Loch Morar and contains more fresh water than all the lakes in England and Wales combined!

'Awesome Scenery And Open Roads'

More of the stunning Scottish countryside

Lovely scenery all around and it's sunny for most of the day. I ask a lady in the tourist shop for a postcard with a photo of Nessie on it but they seem to have run out, although there are lots of plastic Plesiosaurs in a giant bin. To be honest though I doubt there are enough fish and seals in the loch to support a huge dinosaur so maybe 'Nessie' is a giant eel or a Greenland shark. Who knows? It's a great story anyway.

'Monster Spotting'

Derek shy about showing off his knees

On we cycled before stopping at Invermorriston to look at the waterfalls and a lovely old Thomas Telford bridge. Then up a very, very steep hill but it's worth it as we get eight miles of downhill the other side as we coast to Beauly in record time, reaching 38 mph at one point. A superb ride, only spoiled (for a brief second) by some clown who yelled out of his white van window nearly giving me and Derek a cardiac. Fair enough I thought but just wished he'd had the decency to pull over for thirty seconds so I could have beaten the shit out of him!

We push on and thanks to good weather and our speedy descent we've reached our destination with time to burn. A quick conflab and we decide to push on to Dingwall (the drug capital of the North we're told). As if... It's a lovely place although for some reason the government has dumped a load of Kurdish refugees there in a huge hotel? The locals are not happy, and there's plenty of talk about crime and filth on the streets. I'd say the fact there are so many all in one place probably doesn't help assimilation. We then try another hotel but that is full of OAPs from a number of coach trips.

At last we find the best little B&B in town (well, just out of town actually) with really lovely owners, who even oil our bikes for us in the morning! Shame they couldn't do the same for our knees. A cracking seventy-five miles today.

Out for a beer (and why not?) we find a weird kind of discount in the chinkies on my sausages, gravy and chips and head for The Mallard pub as it's pub quiz night and everybody whose anybody is there we're told. In fact I think everybody in the town apart from the Kurds were there. Now the really weird thing about this fab pub was that they have their beer garden actually on the train station platform. Not an old abandoned train station platform mind you, but an actual, working train station platform with trains and everything! I couldn't help thinking that this idea must have caused a few accidents over the years.

Cycling Stats

Start: 7:30am
Distance: 74.74 miles
Total Distance: 826.17 miles
Average Speed: 11.3 mph
Fastest Speed: 38.6 mph
Cycling Time: 6 hrs 30 mins
Finish: 6:30pm
Beers: 4

Day Thirteen
Thursday 14th July 2005
Dingwall to Tongue

A lie in for once. Like I said, a lovely B&B and a really nice couple. Breakie is very good too and we're soon on the road, into the drizzle again with sore knees and a sore bum.

A good Westerly wind sees us whizz past the oil rigs at Cromaty Firth before we head inland to Ardgay (then Bonar Bridge) for a cup of tea and a sticky cake in a roadside café there.

We pedal on, like true explorers now, stop for dinner at Lairg (at the Nipp Inn), have a lovely burger and chips and we're out into the wilderness with a few warnings from the locals.

'Not much after here, make sure you don't break down,' we're warned.

Me and Derek exchange looks with each other, then our heads slowly turn to my bike before we gulp in unison.

'You've been reading our diaries,' I replied.

So after far too many adjustments of our tight shorts, and a few pleading, begging, praying glances at my back wheel we put foot to pedal and pushed off.

A few minutes in, with the town receding in the distance behind us, I wondered what the fuss was all about. The day turned into one of the best bits of the whole trip as we sailed along with the wind. Uphill, downhill, effortlessly cruising through this beautiful barren landscape. Huge mountains in the distance, forestry plantations, moorland, heather and just the whistle of the wind in our helmets. Excellent bimbling territory for some future walking trips and great cycling country. Remote and just wonderful.

We don't see a soul for ages but the reason for this is quite sinister of course. The Highland Clearances (or the 'expulsion of the Gael') was the forced displacement during the 18th and 19th Centuries of a significant number of people from traditional land tenancies in the Scottish Highlands, where they had practised small-scale agriculture. It resulted from enclosures of common lands and a change from farming to sheep raising, an agricultural revolution largely carried out by hereditary aristocratic landowners - the Tory bastards! A Highland Clearance has been defined as 'an enforced simultaneous eviction of all families living in a given area such as an entire glen'.

The Clearances are particularly notorious as a result of the brutality of many evictions at short notice. The cumulative effect of the Clearances devastated the cultural landscape of Scotland in a way that did not happen in other areas of Britain; the effect of the Clearances was to destroy much of the Gaelic culture and resulted in significant emigration of Highlanders to the coast, the Scottish Lowlands, and further afield to North America and Australasia.

Even now there is much controversy over land ownership in Scotland as 432 people own half of the land - the single most concentrated pattern of private ownership in the Western world.

I can't help think about the tyrant Robert Mugabe in Zimbabwe and how he's stolen land from white farmers to give to his friends and keep himself in power. The land is ruined now and the 'bread basket' of Africa is turning to desert. All we see is forestry though so guess someone is still making money from the land here.

'Stopped For A Cuppa'

The Crask Inn, Lairg

If you take Britain as a whole, more than a third of our land is still in the hands of a tiny group of aristocrats. In fact just 36,000 individuals - only 0.6 per cent of the population - own 50% of rural land!

Eventually we arrive at the Crask Inn, which is literally in the middle of nowhere. We stopped for a cuppa, chat to the shy, English, ex-army guy who seems to live here and then decide to leave him to his solitude and his lack of sense of humour and ride on.

Soon after, at Loch Loyal, I spot a black Water Vole (quite rare and a great spot!), although I think our host at Tongue didn't believe me - the cheeky sod. Perhaps I should have told him I was a zoologist sooner?

'Taking My Wheel For A Sightseeing Tour Of North Scotland'

I Love Scotland

We push on along huge, long, winding downhills, stunning scenery, high mountains (that we pass between rather than over) and large rolling moors. This is brilliant. So much better than going up the coast via the 'Inverness' route.

Then the clouds close in and the weather starts to turn a little cooler. We stop to look around and can't see a single person, farmhouse or anything! It's awesome and I love it!

We pedal on, with no idea how far we have to go, feeling slightly disorientated by the vast open spaces. Then eventually we see the village of Tongue below us and breathe a sigh of relief at making it. A great eighty mile ride.

We stay at an old manse (which is lovely) but the Englishman who runs it charges us £5 for a short lift into town which I thought a bit steep seeing as we're doing this ride for charity etc. Isn't it funny how some people are so kind whilst others can be such tight, miserable gits? Maybe he didn't like me correcting him on all his animal facts that he got wrong?

Anyway, we downed a few pints (we'd deserved it) and ate some lovely venison sausages in the pub. Derek made a mobile phone call from the car park and noticed when he walked around he got cut off. He asked the Polish girl working inside (in Polish, because Derek speaks Polish) why this was and without batting an eyelid she answers him (in Polish) while she stands behind a bar in a Scottish pub on the northern most coast of the UK in the middle of nowhere and says you have to stand in the middle of the car park to get a signal - more surrealism for me...

Sue phoned and moaned about how naughty Eve had been. I wasn't surprised. We walked home rather than give the *sais* another fiver and later, when we're safely tucked up in bed we think of home, our families and start to contemplate the end of our journey - tomorrow.

Cycling Stats

Start: 8:30am
Distance: 80.70 miles
Total Distance: 906.87 miles
Average Speed: 11.8 mph
Fastest Speed: 36.1 mph
Cycling Time: 6 hrs 44 mins
Finish: 6:45pm
Beers: 3

Day Fourteen
Friday 15th July 2005
Tongue to John o' Groats

Our last day of cycling and the winds are with us (sort of, they're NW). We set off downhill, then up, then down, then up - it's like Cornwall all over again! Eventually the road flattens out and we stop for tea at the Halledale Inn (a pub with a campsite) to shelter from a spot of rain.

Back in the saddle we cycle past Dounreay Nuclear power station and have the shock of our lives when looking at a field full of sheep. Two of them are llamas! Could they just be llamas or are they the product of some hideous, secret government experiment? Guess we'll never know...

Dounreay used to be the site of two nuclear establishments, for the development of prototype fast breeder reactors and submarine reactor testing since the 1950s. Not sure why the government decided to put it as far away from London, Westminster and the Queen as they did but surely it was nothing to do with safety concerns.

However, in September 1998, a safety audit of the plant was published by the Health and Safety Executive and the Scottish Environment Protection Agency. The results were damning and 143 recommendations were made. In November that year, the UKAEA announced a proposed timetable for accelerated decommissioning, reducing the original schedule from 100 years to forty - sixty years. The cost was estimated at around £4 billion. Guess they found llamas too.

We pass through Thurso, which is quite pretty, albeit touristy, then move on.

We stop for a pint of lager in a freezing cold beer garden about seven miles out of our final destination and we go over the whole trip. Derek gets his bottle of Scotch whisky out so we can warm up.

'Well, we're nearly there,' says Derek.

'Bloody wheel.'

'Great ride I reckon, I've really enjoyed it' he adds.

'Rip-off bloody Britain!'

'Wasn't sure we'd do it but what a buzz!' says Derek.

'Fancy charging us five quid for a ride into town, some people!'

'Come on then...'

'Yeh, I loved it as well,' I say with a grin.

The last bit is easy and when we finally sweep into John o' Groats there is a hail of flash photography, there's even a BBC Wales van there to greet us! The local police have erected barriers but are still having difficulty holding back the huge crowds that have amassed to cheer us on. Even the American tourists from Loch Ness, the coaches full of geriatrics from Dingwall, the little old lady who had the cardiac at the bus stop... everyone is there. Yeh, in my dreams. The place looks deserted.

A few cars try to finish us off, a few random lost tourists walk in front of our bikes but no, nothing.

No one gives a shit that we've buggered our knees for years to come and have achieved something truly amazing considering our extensive planning and preparation (not) and... ah well... nothing for it... pub?

'Is It Downhill If We Cycle Back?'

The beer mat planning paid off

John o' Groats is a tiny village in Caithness, in the far north of Scotland. It lies on Britain's northeastern tip, and is popular with tourists as one end of the longest distance between two inhabited British points, with Land's End in Cornwall lying 876 miles to the southwest. It is not quite the most northerly point on the island of Britain though as nearby Dunnet Head is further north.

John o' Groats is 690 miles from London, 280 miles from Edinburgh and 670 miles from Cardiff.

We arrive at 5:00pm ish after sixty-two miles and head for the famous signpost. We hope there isn't another lazy man we have to pay but fortunately Scotland is far more charitable. We take a few photos, talk to some people getting on ferries to Orkney, visit the gift shop where Derek kindly buys me a small (very small I might add) bottle of Land's End to John o' Groats whisky with a map of the UK on it and then wonder what to do next.

'How many miles is that then Dave?'

'Nine hundred and seventy, nearly,' I reply.

'Mmm?'

'No.'

'What?'

'I know what you're thinking. No way!'

'We could easily do thirty miles in this car park,' says Derek.

'OMG, it's your fault anyway.'

'Mine? Why?'

'You choose the route. You should have added it up better.'

'What? Like Glastonbury...'

Then, just as we think about trying to find the hotel we booked for our last night we turn around and who should be walking across the car park but our fellow Ponty Bimblers - Alun and Mark. They couldn't have timed it better!

A few more photos at the signpost (I reckon it's cheating if you haven't actually cycled or walked it though) and then we head for the Seaview Hotel.

Even though they've had a couple of months to book a room Alun and Mark thought it best to just drive the length of the UK, stop off for a breakfast of fresh salmon, then reach the end of the line and hope for the best. Unlike our meticulous planning (cast your mind back to the beer mat) our 'support crew' have not only decided to just 'appear' but have also neglected Derek's specific instructions to book a large people carrier or van (or even a car with a roof rack) and instead picked the fastest, sportiest model available from the car hire firm to ensure they had comfort and speed driving up to 'rescue' us.

'Where's my bike rack Alun?' asked Derek.

'Oh, I wondered what that was?' said Alun.

'Oh Jesus H Christ mun!'

'I couldn't be arsed to be honest,' came the reply.

Derek's retort was slightly less restrained but needless to say he was not happy. We'd had enough problems with taking wheels off bikes for a lifetime!

Meanwhile, at the reception of the Seaview Hotel...

'Nae rooms tonight laddie,' says the hotel owner.

'Oh crap,' says Mark.

'Sorry lads.'

'Aye I know, but we've come so far buttie, we'll just sleep on the floor eh?' says Alun.

'That's nae allowed.'

'Yeh, it'll be fine. I can slip you a few quid and we're gonna drink a shedload of beer tonight and have food, you know it makes sense,' continued Alun, who I'm sure has sold sand to the Arabs in a previous lifetime.

'OK then.'

So, pub it was. And boy did we have a thirst! Two weeks worth in fact. And that is a fact. The first bar bill is £80 (not including the pizza's at midnight) so you get a rough idea of how many beers we sank.

'Call Yourself A Support Crew!'

Only nine or ten pints in...

We knew we'd be there for the night so to make things easier for the barman we asked for a tab.

'Nae bother,' he replied, 'I doubt you'll drink as much as our footie team over there.'

'Really?' said Mark, sensing a challenge of his own.

John o' Groats is home to two football clubs: John o' Groats and John O Groats Juniors. John o' Groats FC is an amateur team that plays in the top flight of Caithness Amateur Football; it also enters a team into the Winter 7s which are played in Thurso. They also have the distinction of being the most northerly clubs on the island of Great Britain. One of the teams was sat opposite us in the bar but the whole team couldn't drink as much beer as us four though.

The second tab was almost as big, but after we paid that off the barman thought it best if we just paid for each round from then on. Several pints of 'heavy' later it was time to sample the local whisky. Then things went rapidly downhill (is that a cycling joke?).

'Did You Hear About Paddy And Murphy...'

Still early days yet...

Alun is pointing and dribbling.

'Look Dave. Derek wants to fight Mark for more whisky.'

'Oh dear.'

'I want to play pool again,' says Derek swinging a pool cue around the room like a mad clansman.

'Derek, you can't play pool,' says Mark.

'Yes, yes, yes I do... why not?'

'Because you can't stand up or see,' Mark calmly informs my uncoordinated, extremely agitated cycling partner.

'OK,' says Derek as he collapses into his seat again.

We eventually persuade him it's best not to play pool seeing as he can't stand up or see then start to repeat ourselves a few times. (Get it?)

'Late But Still Light'

John o' Groats

Somehow we find our room and make bedfall at 2:00am with Mark snoring loudly on the floor and acting as a draft excluder with his back wedged up against the door. We know this because the next two days he complains constantly that it's our fault that they drove all this way and we didn't organise a bed for them. Alun takes most of Derek's double bed doing his starfish impression in between farting for Wales, while I have a funny little airing cupboard in the corner of the room. As always I open the curtains and windows wide and forget to close them before going to sleep then wonder why I can't sleep with all the noise, cold and light.

Before we went to bed I think I must have wandered outside because the last photo we have is of the beautiful horizon, taken about half past ten at night I believe. Being so far north the summer sun only barely falls below the horizon before rising again a few hours later. A stunning view and a fitting end to a great trip.

Cycling Stats

Start: 9:00am
Distance: 62.83 miles
Total Distance: 969.70 miles
Average Speed: 11.3 mph
Fastest Speed: 37.2 mph
Cycling Time: 5 hrs 31 mins
Finish: 5:10pm
Beers: 20 or more

Day Fifteen
Saturday 16th July
John o' Groats to Glasgow (by car)

Awake at 4:00am (bloody noisy seagulls again), so just two hours kip, but we manage to lie in until 8:00am when they serve breakie.

I order the four of us a huge breakfast each. I eat mine, ask Mark for £12 for his, then eat his too 'cos he isn't hungry. He's never let me forget that the £12 he paid for a cup of tea was the most expensive brew he's ever had. And he's been to Venice.

We somehow manage to dismantle enough of our trusty bikes and cram them into the boot of the, frankly, inadequate car. Alun & Mark take turns to drive us home from Scotland with a hire car kindly donated by Europcar. However a detour via the mountains, deserted cottages and a hot soup at the Crask Inn means time is moving faster than us.

'Déjà vu,' says Derek.

As the barren countryside whizzes by I jabber away about rewilding Britain for an hour or so.

'The reintroduction of the wolf to the Scottish Highlands was first proposed in the late 1960s. They did it in Jellystone in 1995 with the grey wolf.'

'Won't they just eat the deer though?' asks Derek.

'Yeh, but it saves culling them. Anyway I think it's the EU farming subsidies that people need to look at, and we need to please the Scottish government.'

'Are they up for it?' asked Alun.

'I think it's still controversial. Land owners, the bloody royals, farmers, tourists, there's a lot of interested parties.'

'Cyclists?' laughs Mark.

We stop at the 'Nessie Centre' to see if they've had any new postcards in, but still no luck.

'Déjà vu,' says Derek.

Mark simulates a pornographic act with his legs straddling the poor, giant model of the monster in the car park.

'I don't know why we bring him?' Alun says.

The long drive seems longer by car than it was by bike.

Mark takes over the moaning from me, in between sharing his bowel motion stories.

'It's like the 470!' he exclaims.

Alun quickly becomes an expert at giving descriptive hand signals to caravans that hog the road doing 40 mph and Derek and I are glad we have pillows and sleeping bags rammed up against us in the tiny backseat of the car to act as would-be airbags should we hurtle off the mountain what with Alun's increasingly erratic rallying-style of driving.

We only just make Glasgow by 9:00pm.

'It's a big place this Scotland' says Mark.

We check into a Travel Inn, where Alun talks the receptionist into giving us another discount, and are soon out on the town.

It's Saturday night and we're in Glasgow - one of the best cities in the UK for a beer. We do manage a few nice pubs but a couple of takeaways later we're so tired we even pass up the luxury of a lap dancing bar opposite the hotel to fall fast asleep. I share a room with Alun who keeps waking me up to tell me to watch the James Bond film with him.

'Déjà vu,' I say.

Day Sixteen
Sunday 17th July
Glasgow to Pontypridd (by car)

Up early Sunday and drive back to 'Ponty' for a brai and some beers out the back with a few friends and family.

We do a quick summary for the women...

We had good days and bad days although no day could be described as easy. We lost miles on two days (Church Stretton & Crawford - due to a strong headwind and bike problems on both days). The hardest thing was cycling into the wind and my crappy Dawes wheels. The best thing was Scotland's scenery, the wildlife, the kind people and the downhills when we had the wind with us! We covered a total of 969.70 miles at an average speed of 11.06 mph. The fastest I went was 38.60 mph down quite a few hills, although Derek certainly went much quicker (well over 40 mph) because he is mental on a bike.

And finally, a worth-mentioning footnote regards this type of endurance event. Both myself and Derek ate like sumo wrestlers over the two weeks and had at least a couple of beers each night. We both lost close to a stone in weight.

More information to follow...

Towns & Villages

<u>Note</u>:

Since writing this book I've seen lots of other 'LEJOG' books / guides that either include detailed GPS information, a myriad of maps or instructions of where to turn left (or right), where to fix your bike, where to stay, where to drink, where to pick up nerdy women (OK maybe not) and so on... This is all very well and good but surely the point of any trip like this is the unknown, the adventure, the not knowing what's around the corner (literally), so that is why this account is just that, an honest write-up of a great trip that two lads took way back in the mists of time. We didn't do much planning, we just went, and our adventure was all the more exciting and enjoyable for that! However, if you do want to repeat what we did just get a map and cycle through the towns and villages below - you don't need anything else. You'll see the same stuff (minus the usual shifting sands), you'll encounter different weather and different people, pass the same landscape, although some of the pubs will be shut by now and when your bike breaks down you'll find new ways to repair it and carry on. So here is where we ended up going:

Day 1
Places we passed through...
Land's End, Sennen, Kelynack, Bosavern, St.Just, Botallack, Carnyorth, Trewellard, Bodjewyan, Portmeor, Treer, Zennor, Trendrine, Hellesveor, St.Ives, Carbis Bay, Hayle, Gwithian, Portreath, Bridge, Cambrose, Porthtowan, St.Agnes, Trevelas

Downs, Perranport, Goonhavern, Rejerrah,
Rosecliston, Trevemper, Treninnick, Newquay

Day 2
Places we passed through...
Porth, St.Columb Minor, St.Columb Major, Gluvian,
No Mans Land, Wadebridge, Trevanson, St.Kew
Highway, Knightsmill, Helstone, Camelford, Trefrew,
Trewassa, Hallworthy, Cold Northcott, Pipers Pool,
Tregadillet, Launceston, Liftdown, Tinhay, Lewdown,
Lobhillcross, Bridstowe, Forde, Okehampton

Day 3
Places we passed through...
Bow, Clannaborough, Copplestone, Crediton,
Shobroke, Little Silver, West Raddon, Thorverton, Up
Exe, Silverton, Bradnininch, Colebrook, Cullompton,
Willand, Waterloo Cross, Prescott, Culmstock,
Woodgate, Nichlashayne, Red Ball, White Ball,
Rockwell Green, Wellington, West Buckland,
Rumwell, Taunton, Monkton Heathfield, West
Monkton, Durston, West Lyng, Lyng, Burrow Bridge,
Othery, Greylake, Greinton, Pedwell, Berhill, Walton,
Street, Northover, Glastonbury

Day 4
Places we passed through...
Northload Bridge, Southway, Coxley, Wells, West
Horrignton, Emborough, Chilcompton, Midsomer
Norton, Radstock, Clandown, Peasedown St.John,
Odd Down, Bath, Bathampton, Batheaston,
Northend, Upper Wraxall, North Wraxall, Nettleton,
Burton, Acton Turville, Luckington, Sopworth,

Didmarton, Oldbury on the hill, Leighterton,
Kingscote, Nymphsfield, Frocester, Middle Street,
Eastington, Whitminster, Morton Valence, Framilode
Putloe, Quedgeley, Hempstead, Gloucester

Day 5
Places we passed through...
Over, Maisemore, Twigworth, Hartpury, Corse,
Staunton, Redmarley, Playley Green, Bromsberrow,
Newton, Ledbury, Saplow, Catley, Castle Frome,
Bishops Frome, Munderford Stocks, Munderford
Row, Bromyard, Edwyn Ralph, Collington, Pie
Corner, Bank Street, Kyre Park, Nineveh, Kyre
Wood, Tenbury Wells, Greete, Caynsham, Ludlow,
Bromfield, Onibury, Stokesay, Craven Arms, Halford,
Strefford, Upper Affcot, Little Stretton, Church
Stretton

Day 6
Places we passed through...
All Stretton, Leebotwood, Dorrington, Stapleton,
Lythbank, Bayston Hill, Meole Brace, Shrewsbury,
Albrighton, Preston Gubbals, Harmer Hill, Alderton,
Wem, Creamore Bank, Edstaston, Quina Brook,
Coton, Steel Heath, Tilstock, Whitchurch, Bickley
Moss, Croxton Green, Ridley Green, Peckforton,
Spurton, Bunbury Heath, Tiverton, Tarporley,
Cotebrook, Delamere, Cuddington, Blackmere,
Hatchmere, Commonside, Fivecrosses, Overton,
Newtown, Frodsham, Sutton Weaver, Weston,
Runcorn, West Bank, Hale Bank, Hale, Speke

Day 7
Places we passed through...
Halewood, Tarback Green, Huyton, Whiston Lane
End, Whiston, Prescott, Ecclestone, St.Helens,
Crank, Kings Moss, Crawford, Up Holland, Roby Mill,
Bank Top, Darlton Lees, Holland, Appleby Bridge,
Robin Hood, Mossley Lea, Wrightington Bar, Heskin
Green, Ecclestone Green, Ecclestone, Leyland,
Farrington, Lower, Penwortham, Preston, Fulwood,
Cadley, Snaroe Green, Broughton, Newsham,
Barton, Bilsborrow, Brock, Catteral, Bowgreave
Bonds, Garstang, Forton, Pottersbrook, Galgate,
Ellel, Scotforth, Lancaster

Day 8
Places we passed through...
Skerton, Slyne, Bolton Town End, Bolton Le Sands,
Carnforth, Burton in Kendal, Clawthorpe, Farleton,
Millness, Crooklands, Endmoor, Summerlands,
Kendal, Garth Row, Watchgate, Forest Hall,
Bretherdale Head, Shap, Hackthorpe, Lowther
Clifton, Eamont Bridge, Penrith, Plumpton Head,
Plumpton, Old Town, High Heskett, Low Heskett,
Scalesceugh, Carleton, Upperby, Carlisle

Day 9
Places we passed through...
Kingtown, Todhills, Gretna, Gretna Green,
Springfield, Kirkpartick Fleming, Lirlebridge,
Ecclefechan, Lockerbie, Nethercleugh,
Johnstonebridge, Beattock, Backlaw, Nether
Houcieugh, March, Elvanfoot, Bellfield, Crawford

Day 10
Places we passed through...
Abington, Urdington, Happendon, Lesmahagow, Kirkmuirhill, Blackwood, Strutherhill, Shawsburn, Larkhall, Allanton, Ferniegair, Hamilton, Blantyre, Flemingan, Camuslang, Rutherglen, Glasgow, Partick, Anniesland, Clydebank, Parkhall, Duntocher, Old Kilpatrick, Bowling, Milton, Dumbarton, Townend, Castlehill, Alexandria, Balloch, Arden, Aldochlay, Luss, Inverbe, Tarbet

Day 11
Places we passed through...
Ardluilnverarnan, Crianlarich, Tyndrum, Bridge of Orchy, Glencoe, Ballachulish, North Ballachulish, Onich, Ardgour, Coruanan Lodge, Druimarbin, Auchintare, Fort William

Day 12
Places we passed through...
Spean Bridge, Tronena, Glenfintaig Lodge, Invergloy, Laggan, Invergarry, Aberchalder Lodge, Newtown, Fort Augustus, Invermorriston, Lenie, Lewiston, Drumnadrochit, Milton, Tomnacross, Balblair, Beauly, Tomich, Ardnagrask, Muir of Ord, Conan Bridge, Maryburgh, Dingwall

Day 13
Places we passed through...
Evanton, Alness, Achandunie, Aulnamain Inn, Upper Ardchronie, Kincardine, Ardgay, Bonar Bridge, Invershin, Lairg, Crask Inn, Altnaharra, Loyal Lodge, Tongue

Day 14
Places we passed through...
Coldbackie, Bettyhill, Armadale, Strathy, Melvich, Reaylsauld, Dounreay, Buldoo, Bridge of Forss, Thurso, Murkle, Castletown, Dunnet, Mey, Gills, Cannisbay, Huna, John o' Groats

List of our sponsors

R.H. Jeffs & Rowe
Alun / Mark
Debbie Davies
Maesycoed Motors
Clwb-Y-Bont
Richard Holland
Cil Con Club
All bike shops (en route)
Lucozade
Europcar
Kellsboro Hotel
Paul - the bouncy castle man
Jazz cafe owner, Bath
John Sykes (Luckington PO)
Fred of CWA Cycles
Mark Lancaster of Jack Davies Cycles
Preston Bike Shop
Scottish man in Halfords, Dumfries
Glasgow local lads
Hotel staff, Seaview Hotel

We raised approx. £750 for Ty-Hafan - the children's hospice.

Records

Land's End to John o' Groats is the classic journey for those wishing to travel the whole length of Great Britain.

The traditional distance by road is 874 miles and takes most cyclists ten to fourteen days.

The official Road Records Association record for a rider on a conventional bicycle is 44 hours, 4 minutes and 20 seconds, set by Gethin Butler in 2001.

The oldest person to cycle from Land's End to John O'Groats is Tony Rathbone who was aged 81 years and 162 days when he completed the journey on 21 May 2014.

The record for running the route is nine days and two hours, by Andi Rivett.

Off-road walkers typically walk about 1,200 miles and take two or three months for the expedition.

The two much-photographed signposts indicate the traditional distance at each end, although we did 970 miles and missed the first signpost 'cos the nasty man had taken the place names home to bed with him.

Although we took two weeks we felt we did alright and completed the route in good speed, especially without any training. However the fastest passage between the two points was made in 1988 by a McDonnell F-4K Phantom in a time of 46 minutes 44 seconds so maybe we weren't that fast after all.

References

Bike Britain by Paul Slater, paperback, 160 pages, Epic New Zealand Ltd (1 Jan. 2002).

A few printed maps of the UK, which Derek printed off, then threw away when we'd cycled off that page.

Evil Google so I could check my facts regards towns and history stuff when writing this account up.

Dave Lewis is from Cilfynydd, South Wales. He has always lived in Wales except for a year in Kenya.

He has published many books, although this is his first travel book.

He is founder and organiser of The Welsh Poetry Competition, an international competition which seeks to encourage and nurture talented writers that have been overlooked by the arts establishment in Wales.

If you liked this paperback and could find five minutes to leave a positive review on Amazon, Dave would be thrilled. And please pass the link on to anyone who fancies jumping on a bike to do the same ride, because as we proved, any idiot can do it if they put their minds to it. And lastly, good luck to anyone that does - it was real.

For more information about the author and to see his other work please visit his web site –

www.david-lewis.co.uk

By the same author:

Fiction:
Layer Cake © 2009
Urban Birdsong © 2010
Sawing Fallen Logs For Ladybird Houses © 2011
Ctrl-Alt-Delete © 2011
Haiku © 2012
Raising Skinny Elephants © 2013
Roadkill © 2013
iCommand © 2015

Edited:
Welsh Poetry Competition Anthology © 2011

Non-Fiction:
Photography Composition © 2014
Land's End to John o' Groats © 2015

Websites:
www.david-lewis.co.uk
www.davelewisphotography.co.uk
www.welshpoetry.co.uk
www.publishandprint.co.uk

23182778R00070

Printed in Great Britain
by Amazon